Civil War Generals of the Confederacy

Other Books in the History Makers Series:

Civil War Generals of the Confederacy

By James P. Reger

Lucent Books
P. O. Box 289011, San Diego, CA 92198-9011

Library of Congress Cataloging-in-Publication Data

Reger, James P.
　　Civil War generals of the Confederacy / by James P. Reger.
　　　　p.　　cm. — (History makers)
　　Summary: Focuses on the military careers of influential generals of the
Confederacy during the Civil War.
　　ISBN 1-56006-359-9 (lib : alk. paper)
　　1. Generals—Confederate States of America—Biography—Juvenile
literature.　2. Confederate States of America.　Army—Biography—
Juvenile literature.　3. United States—History—Civil War, 1861–
1865—Biography—Juvenile literature.　[1. Generals.　2. Confederate
States of America.　Army—Biography.　3. United States—History—
Civil War, 1861–1865—Biography.]　I. Title.　II. Series.
E467.R45　1999
973.7'13'0922—dc21   98-36191
                                                                    CIP
                                                                    AC

CONTENTS

FOREWORD

The literary form most often referred to as "multiple biography" was perfected in the first century A.D. by Plutarch, a perceptive and talented moralist and historian who hailed from the small town of Chaeronea in central Greece. His most famous work, *Parallel Lives*, consists of a long series of biographies of noteworthy ancient Greek and Roman statesmen and military leaders. Frequently, Plutarch compares a famous Greek to a famous Roman, pointing out similarities in personality and achievements. These expertly constructed and very readable tracts provided later historians and others, including playwrights like Shakespeare, with priceless information about prominent ancient personages and also inspired new generations of writers to tackle the multiple biography genre.

The Lucent History Makers series proudly carries on the venerable tradition handed down from Plutarch. Each volume in the series consists of a set of six to eight biographies of important and influential historical figures who were linked together by a common factor. In *Rulers of Ancient Rome*, for example, all the figures were generals, consuls, or emperors of either the Roman Republic or Empire; while the subjects of *Fighters Against American Slavery*, though they lived in different places and times, all shared the same goal, namely the eradication of human servitude. Mindful that politicians and military leaders are not (and never have been) the only people who shape the course of history, the editors of the series have also included representatives from a wide range of endeavors, including scientists, artists, writers, philosophers, religious leaders, and sports figures.

Each book is intended to give a range of figures—some well known, others less known; some who made a great impact on history, others who made only a small impact. For instance, by making Columbus's initial voyage possible, Spain's Queen Isabella I, featured in *Women Leaders of Nations*, helped to open up the New World to exploration and exploitation by the European powers. Unarguably, therefore, she made a major contribution to a series of events that had momentous consequences for the entire world. By contrast, Catherine II, the eighteenth-century Russian queen, and Golda Meir, the modern Israeli prime minister, did not play roles of global impact; however, their policies and actions significantly influenced the historical development of both their own countries and their regional neighbors. Regardless of their relative importance in the greater historical scheme, all of the figures chronicled in the History Makers series made contributions to posterity; and their public achievements, as well as what is known about their private lives, are presented and evaluated in light of the most recent scholarship.

In addition, each volume in the series is documented and substantiated by a wide array of primary and secondary source quotations. The primary source quotes enliven the text by presenting eyewitness views of the times and culture in which each history maker lived; while the secondary source quotes, taken from the works of respected modern scholars, offer expert elaboration and/or critical commentary. Each quote is footnoted, demonstrating to the reader exactly where biographers find their information. The footnotes also provide the reader with the means of conducting additional research. Finally, to further guide and illuminate readers, each volume in the series features photographs, a chronology, two bibliographies, and a comprehensive index.

The History Makers series provides both students engaged in research and more casual readers with informative, enlightening, and entertaining overviews of individuals from a variety of circumstances, professions, and backgrounds. No doubt all of them, whether loved or hated, benevolent or cruel, constructive or destructive, will remain endlessly fascinating to each new generation seeking to identify the forces that shaped their world.

"The Man Is Everything"

What makes a general great? Is it his upbringing, his family status, his work habits, his intelligence, his physical strength, his personal courage, or his devotion to his duty? Perhaps it is his academic prowess, his knowledge of history, military theory, or engineering. Certainly, he must be able to keep his army fed, clothed, and supplied while inspiring them to undertake dangerous acts. And he must convince his men that the cause they are fighting for is worth possibly dying for.

All of these factors are building blocks in the general's foundation. The individual comes from the same quarry of personality traits and natural instincts. But any of these building blocks, standing alone or stacked upon each other, fail to make a general great without the mortar required to meld them into extraordinary leadership. The renowned military theorist Alfred von Schlieffen called that mortar *character* and he proclaimed, "The character of the commander is the first thing in winning battles." [1] In a similar vein, no less a conqueror than Napoleon Bonaparte remarked, "When it comes to victory, men are nothing, the man is everything." [2]

The Confederate States of America produced some 425 generals ranging from the worthless to the competent, but only a handful possessed the character to achieve unarguable excellence. Foremost among these were Robert E. Lee, Thomas J. "Stonewall" Jackson, James "Pete" Longstreet, James Ewell Brown (Jeb) Stuart, and Nathan Bedford Forrest. And that same mortar, character, that cemented their individual greatness also cemented them into a group as monumental as Mount Rushmore.

Their nicknames alone suggest the essence of that group. People called Robert E. Lee the "Marble Model" because he seemed to have fewer flaws than a pristine work of statuary. Thomas Jackson earned the name "Stonewall" not only for his defensive stand at First Manassas but for the unyielding fervor with which he drove his men to victory. Lee gave James Longstreet his moniker, the "War Horse," for the stolid general's glacial dependability and the silent command with which he moved mountains

Generals Robert E. Lee (left) and Stonewall Jackson confer for the last time in May 1863 before Jackson is fatally injured. Jackson was one of Lee's most important generals.

and men. J. E. B. Stuart came to be known as "the Cavalier of Dixie" for his swashbuckling derring-do and the pranks he constantly played upon the enemy. And Nathan Bedford Forrest relied upon stark violence and a raging will to earn his sobriquet, "That Devil Forrest."

But can any one man, even one with enough command presence to earn a worthy nickname, really affect an army's performance in battle? Napoleon, the "Little Corporal," thought that he could:

> The personality of the general is indispensible. He is the head, he is the all of an army. The Gauls were not conquered by the Roman Legions, but by Caesar. It was not before the Carthaginian soldiers that Rome was made to tremble, but before Hannibal. It was not the Macedonian phalanx which penetrated India, but Alexander.[5]

Napoleon probably overstated the value of the commander and his character, for he was trying to make a point about himself. Nevertheless, it did take more than just the Confederate foot soldiers to nearly sever the South from the United States. It took this handful of truly influential Rebel generals—Lee, Jackson, Longstreet, Stuart, and Forrest—to conceive, believe, and very nearly achieve the vision and dream of an independent Southern nation. And whether one calls it character, personality, presence, or instinct, these five men possessed and manifested it in abundance and, in the final measure, that was what made them great.

CHAPTER 1

Brothers of Different Mothers

On April 14, 1861, in Charleston, South Carolina, church bells rang, cannons pounded, pistol fire crackled up into the magnolia-scented skies. Union-occupied Fort Sumter had fallen. The South might soon be free at last and her citizens from South Carolina to Texas were frolicking like children at the prospect. Liquor flowed like a river. Blustering speeches resounded from balconies. Ladies whirled children and gentlemen slapped backs. Were it not for the aged and infirmed, all of Dixie would have been dancing in the firelit streets. The diarist Mary Chesnut recorded,

> In the afternoon, I drove around the Battery. We were in an open carriage. What a scene! The very liveliest crowd I think I ever saw. Everyone talking at once, all glasses still turned on the grim old fort. This is a grand frolic! The soldiers' camp is in a fit of horseplay.[4]

And why not? For two hundred years, Southerners had considered themselves a different race from the Yankees to the North. There were no televisions or movies or music groups or fads for North and South to share and, as a result, they had never really established any sense of a common background. They had grown so irreconcilably apart in terms of their visions for America that, by 1861, the snowy North and the steamy South possessed cultures critically incompatible with one another.

When Yankee Doodle Came to Town

Northerners tended small farms and fished icy New England waters. They were artisans and merchants who sought banking capital to invest in emerging factories from Massachusetts to New York to Illinois. The factories drew young women laborers at first and then poor male immigrants escaping hardships in Europe. They also attracted struggling white men already in the country. At their worst, the factory owners paid children a few pennies a

Manufacturing plants in the North such as this starch factory in Oswego, New York, made up the North's large industrial base. The North's reliance on industry and the South's reliance on agriculture made the two regions of the nation increasingly different.

day to work dangerous machines for long, exhausting shifts and then sent them home to sleep for a few hours before returning to the same risky grind. At their best, factories fostered the development of a semiskilled, comparatively well paid technical or blue-collar class which, when coupled with office or white-collar workers, formed the fastest growing middle class in the world.

Wherever these workers gathered to earn their wages, merchants, grocers, and businessmen also congregated to serve them. Thus, villages, towns, and cities popped up like toadstools throughout the first half of the nineteenth century. Railroads and canals supported commerce and travel between consumers who needed manufactured goods and factories that needed raw materials. Before long, the North had generated an interdependent economic network that made and delivered some of the most technologically advanced products in the world. And that interdependent network yielded another significant by-product. The people in the North began to see themselves less as New Yorkers or Pennsylvanians or Ohioans and more as Americans. The same could not be said of the South, where state loyalties still superseded national ones.

Way Down South in Dixie

Using both slave and free labor, some manufacturing plants sprouted up in states such as Virginia, Kentucky, Tennessee, and the Carolinas. Writes one historian,

The most important of the early textile manufacturers was William Gregg of South Carolina. He worked hard to weaken the southern prejudice against manufacturing and made his own plant a model of benevolent paternalism. The people who worked for him lived in company houses, traded at the company store, and worshipped in company-owned churches. Children under twelve were required to attend the school Gregg built for them.[5]

But, as a rule, most Southerners still preferred the slow-paced, easygoing agricultural lifestyle to the hustled bustle of factory work. Consequently, technology grew at a fraction of the pace that it did up North.

Plantation owners take a walk through their lush grounds. Wealthy Southerners knew that their lifestyle would deteriorate quickly without the free labor of thousands of slaves.

The consequent lack of finished goods manufactured in the South meant that Southerners had to buy them either from factories in the North or those in England (which charged less than Northern plants). Since both the Northern and English markets wanted Southern cotton and tobacco, a lucrative trade matured. But even that trade led to one of the problems that drove an immovable wedge between the two diverging Americas.

Northern factory owners wanted to monopolize the trade with the South so they devised a way to increase the cost of Southern commerce with England. The Northern politicians passed tariffs (import taxes) on all manufactured goods coming from England. It then cost the Southerners more to buy English products, which had the Yankee tariff attached, than to buy Northern ones, which did not. According to one observer, "Southerners soon concluded that besides increasing the cost of nearly everything they bought, high tariff duties would limit the foreign market for southern staples by inhibiting international exchange."[6] For these reasons, the Southerners detested having to pay the Northerners more and more for their finished goods. They strove all the harder to gain more control over their own economic destiny, without the tariffs imposed by the Yankees.

Different Classes, Different Masses

Disagreement over what constituted a middle class further differentiated the drifting halves of America. Northerners were fond of claiming that there was no middle class in the South, just a minority of plantation owners ruling over an ocean of poverty (slaves and so-called poor white trash). They based this opinion on the reports of the few Yankee travelers to the outback of the region who mistook small farms for being ramshackled and beggarly.

In fact, many Southern middle-class farmers did live in casually maintained homesteads, compared with their Northern counterparts who had to put great effort into their dwellings just to survive the winters. But, as an eminent historian writes,

> Nevertheless, small farmers did grow the staple crops and many of them owned a few slaves, often working alongside them in the fields. These yeoman farmers did not seem very remarkable to contemporary chroniclers, but they were the backbone of the South—respectable, hard-working, hospitable, self-reliant, and moderately prosperous.[7]

Necessity clearly placed fewer demands upon the middle-class Southern farmers than on their cold-climed counterparts to the

North. By and large, Southern weather was mild, forest game was plentiful, fish filled the streams, and crops could be grown year-round. Had the yeoman farmers of Mississippi, Alabama, Georgia, and the Carolinas been harder pressed by nature to battle the elements for survival, perhaps they too would have ended up as close-mouthed and industrious as the pent-in New Englanders. But there was no such need so they had more time for shooting, riding, gambling, drinking, and smoking fine Southern tobacco.

The Bungled Burden

The upper classes of the two regions, with their mutual wealth and status, should have been able to achieve some common ground, but that did not happen either. Even when doing business with each other, they never found any mutual links aside from the money, and they had plenty of differences regarding how they ran their operations. Most prominently, aristocrats in the South regarded their workers (slaves) as being so inferior and childlike that they were obliged to care for them twenty-four hours a day for the length of time that they owned them. The planters called this the "white man's burden."

Slaves performed every type of labor for their wealthy owners, from the tedious and backbreaking agricultural tasks like picking cotton, to cooking, sewing, and washing.

Certainly they expected obedience, respect, and honor in return for their patronage and would punish any slave who rebelled. But most slave owners treated their workers passably. Remarkably, one contemporary Northern observer reported that the slaves he saw on a trip to the South were "nearly always adequately clothed, fed, and housed, for only a fool or a sadist would fail to protect such valuable property."[8] And, of course, Southern planters all lived and worked among their slaves in close proximity on the plantation.

Northern upper-class members, as Southerners saw them, often extolled the personal value and natural rights of Southern slaves while showing far less regard for their own employees. Northern business owners often failed to provide their workers with food, housing, clothing, medical care, or job security. Concerning the Southern workforce, most Northern entrepreneurs favored at least a gradual emancipation of the slaves, but few were willing to have them move into their own towns and neighborhoods. Abraham Lincoln himself wanted to send freed slaves to the untamed jungles of Central or South America. His preference acknowledged the dismal fact that blacks would likely not be treated fairly in either the North or the South for at least another century. His words proved prophetic. Few aristocrats in the Northern states or white men in the South would lend any tangible support to the slaves after they gained their freedom.

A War of Words and Votes

By the mid–nineteenth century, the North and the South were more different than the United States and England or Canada and Australia. Both regions possessed economies, societies, and cultures varied enough to stand as two separate and sovereign nations. But until such a split took place, what remained to be decided was which faction would gain dominance over the other and rule the entire country as it suited them (and, conversely, as it did not suit their rival).

The main crucible for this power struggle was the U.S. Congress, which spent thirty years attempting to resolve the ever-widening rift. The goal of the congressmen was to keep the same number of slave and free states in the Union so that neither side could gain a voting advantage over the other. In the Missouri Compromise of 1820, for example, Congress admitted slave Missouri and free Maine at the same time. Texas (slave) entered the Union in 1845 but only with the guarantee that territories expected to be won in the Mexican War would be free (the Wilmot

Proviso). And the Compromise of 1850 allowed California to join the Union as a free state as long as slavery would not be restricted in the Southwestern territories.

The Kansas-Nebraska Act of 1854 sounded like a logical idea at the time. It let the people living in each territory decide for themselves whether or not they wanted to allow slavery. But the plan failed when vicious skirmishing ripped through Kansas and Missouri. Proslavers and antislavers violently attempted to pad the population and the voting rolls within those territories applying for statehood with people of their own persuasion while discouraging any others. The six-year period of prewar brutality spawned "Bleeding Kansas" and a murderous abolitionist named John Brown. After murdering five people in Kansas, Brown attempted to pull off a slave uprising in Harpers Ferry, Virginia (now West Virginia), in 1859 that, while failing, made him a hero in the North.

When the Virginians hanged him for what they saw as his treason, the Northerners made him a martyr and a saint, which pushed many Southerners to the brink of secession. One Virginian said at the time, "I have always been a fervid Union man, but I confess the northern endorsement of the Harpers Ferry outrage has shaken my fidelity."[9]

War became next to inevitable at that point. The rawest of raw nerves for the Southerners had been painfully twanged. Even to moderates in the South, John Brown's raid looked like proof that elements in the North were trying to encourage the slaves to rise up and kill their masters and their families as they lay helpless in their beds. The final thread of union unraveled altogether in 1860 when Abraham Lincoln, long considered to be pro-Northern and opposed to the spread of slavery, was elected president. South Carolina seceded from the Union within a month and the six other deep South states joined her shortly thereafter.

The four upper South states followed after Fort Sumter fell and Lincoln called for seventy-five thousand volunteers to forcibly hold the Southern states in the Union. The compromising was over. The Southerners had created a nation and now they were preparing for an invasion by the "foreign aggressors" from the North. All that remained for them, they thought, was to wait for their military leaders, both at home and returning from assignments with the U.S. Army, to step forward and cast the invaders from their new country. And those military leaders responded with a command style as different from that of the Yankees as anything else that ever separated North and South.

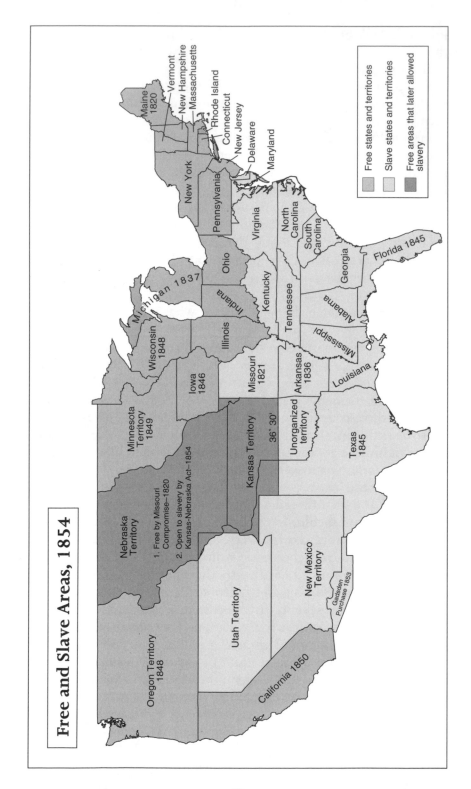

Free and Slave Areas, 1854

Legend:
- Free states and territories
- Slave states and territories
- Free areas that later allowed slavery

Maine 1820
Vermont
New Hampshire
Massachusetts
Rhode Island
Connecticut
New Jersey
Delaware
Maryland
New York
Pennsylvania
Virginia
North Carolina
South Carolina
Georgia
Florida 1845
Ohio
Kentucky
Tennessee
Alabama
Michigan 1837
Indiana
Illinois
Mississippi
Wisconsin 1848
Iowa 1846
Missouri 1821
Arkansas 1836
Louisiana
Minnesota Territory 1849
Kansas Territory
36° 30'
Unorganized territory
Texas 1845
Nebraska Territory

1. Free by Missouri Compromise–1820
2. Open to slavery by Kansas-Nebraska Act–1854

Oregon Territory 1848
Utah Territory
New Mexico Territory
Gadsden Purchase 1853
California 1850

Five "Knights" Heed the Call

Perhaps that style of leadership can best be summed up in one word: chivalry. Originally, chivalry was a code of honorable behavior prescribed for knights during the Middle Ages. It was an attempt to combine the ethics of Christianity with those of the battlefield. The ideals of a chivalrous knight were courage, fighting skill, piety, honor, generosity, and service to his God, his feudal lord, and his lady.

By the time of the Civil War, these ideals had been internalized by all Southern gentlemen but, in particular, by those who had attended military academies. The widespread popularity of the novels by Sir Walter Scott, especially *Ivanhoe,* which romanticized the days of knights and their fair ladies, further popularized the values of chivalry among Southern men. They even led to mock jousting tournaments in which the winners of medieval martial contests placed their chosen damsels on a raised throne or pedestal for the day.

And whether in reenactments or in the everyday lives of Southern gentlemen, the sublimest of courtesies, good manners, and fair play prevailed, at least in theory. Knights in helmets or top hats were expected to respect their enemies, fight for their leaders, and take care of the peons beneath them. Daily, they were to prayerfully rededicate themselves to the defense of their faith, their families, their friends, their followers, and their home as they conceived it to be: their town, county, state, or region, and now the Confederate States of America.

Clearly not even the best-intentioned Southern men could consistently live up to the strict code of chivalry (it is doubtful that many medieval knights did either). But the five leading Confederate generals took the code seriously enough to make a worthy attempt. Robert E. Lee, Thomas J. Jackson, James Longstreet, James Ewell Brown Stuart, and Nathan Bedford Forrest measured up to the ideal about as well as any combat commanders could have. Their efforts are especially noteworthy considering the brutal nature of internecine warfare, that is, battle within a group. And they helped to set the tone for the rest of the Rebel high command.

Ironically, the code that they may have thought elevated them over the Yankees may have also contributed to their losing the war. Their chivalric refusal to adopt the Federals' tactics (devastation of the citizenry, refusal to exchange prisoners, cutting off food and medicine, and similar actions) probably hampered their own prospects for success in what became, despite their gentlemanly honor, a decidedly ungentlemanly war.

19

CHAPTER 2

Robert E. Lee:
More Man than Marble

At the Custis-Lee Mansion in Arlington Heights, Virginia, Colonel Robert Edward Lee slowly paced back and forth through the midnight shadows of his lamp-lit bedroom. He wore a blue, watch-fobbed vest, trousers of the same color bearing a yellow stripe down each leg, and a starched white shirt. Even late in the evening of April 20, 1861, his cravat remained properly tied around his neck although he had allowed himself to take off his U.S. Army coat and drape it over the back of his desk chair. It was, after all, a warm spring evening outside, with wafting breezes carrying in the delicate scents of sweet cherry blossoms, a pleasant break from the pent-up mustiness and fireplace odors of the recent closed-in winter.

The fifty-three-year-old Lee stopped in front of a tall, arched window and ran his hand through his graying hair. He sighed tiredly, gazing upon the distant White House, where the dilemma with which he now grappled had originated. Its current occupant, President Abraham Lincoln, had offered him command of the entire U.S. Army: the assignment of a lifetime, the crowning of a long, illustrious career as a professional military man. So why did it trouble him so deeply to decide whether or not to accept the post?

In a word, it was Virginia: his home, his heritage, his very country as he had often called it. And honor, of course; always there was his inviolate code of honor. Civil war was breaking out across the land. Southerners wanted to secede from the United States and start their own country. Northerners were preparing an invasion to prevent such a rending of the young nation, an invasion that would no doubt begin in his beloved Virginia, now that it had formally joined the seceding Confederate States of America.

Colonel Lee, pensively stroking his salt-and-pepper mustache, turned away from the window and knelt to pray beside the canopied bed. His handsome face, smooth and full cheeked, drooped with sorrow. Anguish furrowed his brow. When he had completed his silent prayer, he arose with a creak and sat at his desk. He picked up his quill pen and dipped it in a bottle of ink. He adjusted the parchment to its proper angle and proceeded to make the most momentous decision of his life. The letter, written to his mentor, General Winfield Scott, read in part:

> I have not been able to make up my mind to raise my hand against my relatives, my children, my home. I therefore resign

When civil war became inevitable, President Lincoln wanted Robert E. Lee (pictured) to command the Union army. Feeling that he could not betray his native South, Lee turned down the offer.

my commission in the Army, and save in defense of my native State, with the sincere hope that I may never be called upon to again draw my sword.[10]

It was an inevitable decision, one predetermined by the earliest and most indelible experiences of his life.

Position Without Wealth

Since January 19, 1807, when Anne Carter Lee and Richard Henry Lee proudly announced the birth of their fourth child, the die had been cast for the boy they named Robert Edward. Both the Lee and Carter families had long been regarded as two of the finest and most powerful clans in Old Virginia. Richard Henry, Robert's father, had achieved a measure of greatness as a cavalry officer during the American Revolution. The ancient patriarch of his mother's family, Charles "King" Carter, was still honored as one of colonial Virginia's most influential founders. Regarding the Lees (two of whom had signed the Declaration of Independence), President George Washington remarked, "I know no country that can produce a family all distinguished as clever men, as our Lees."[11]

However, by the time of Robert's birth, his father, once revered as "Light Horse Harry" for his brave service to George Washington's Continental Army, was financially bankrupt due to imprudent investments in land schemes. Even being elected governor of Virginia had not enriched him. Lee ran from creditors, spent a year in debtors' prison, and finally fled his family responsibilities altogether for the legal sanctuary of British Barbados. His absences had caused the shy and reserved Robert to grow up with a part-time father at best, although, in keeping with the boy's already mature character, he never spoke badly of "Light Horse Harry" and often recounted happy times spent with the playful, childlike man.

With her husband gone, all that remained for Robert's mother, Anne Carter Lee, was to move her children near well-to-do extended family members in Alexandria, Virginia. There, she must have thought, she could at least maintain ties to her family's social status if not its wealth.

It was during this time of devotion to his increasingly ailing mother that Robert "carried the keys," or took over the responsibilities of the household. According to a neighbor, the prematurely serious Robert learned "to practice self-denial and self-control, as well as the strictest economy in all financial concerns."[12] In addition to his more "manly" duties, he cooked, cleaned, and raised his little sister with such maternal tenderness and sensitivity that his mother risked what another more ordinary boy might have considered a disparaging remark. "How can I live without Robert?" she said. "He is both son and daughter to me." [13]

By the age of seventeen, Robert knew that his hopes for a higher education would hinge upon possible scholarships or free educations that might be available to him via public channels. The United States Military Academy at West Point, New York, attracted him due to its free tuition and the promise of an honorable career afterward. Given his outstanding performance in preparatory school, his natural talents in mathematics, and recommendations that included phrases such as "correct and gentlemanly habits, . . . well-versed in Algebra, Euclid [Geometry], and the classics . . . excellent disposition, . . . many talents and attainments, . . . compatible with rules, . . . amiable disposition and irreproachable morals," he gained admittance to "the Point" in 1825. [14]

The Marble Man Emerges

From the beginning, the course of study and training had been designed to weed out the weak and temper the strong. Four hundred cadets entered West Point in 1825; only two hundred graduated four years later. The reason is clear. Few young men could endure four years of waking at dawn, marching for two hours, attending classes all morning, studying independently for two hours, marching for two more hours, studying an additional two hours after that, and then, prior to bedtime, standing outside for final inspection regardless of the weather. Their only breaks came during the three thirty-minute meals of unseasoned potatoes, thin soup, and gruel—sometimes eaten while at full, braced attention. The remarkable fact is not that half of the cadets quit but that any of them endured. But many did and Robert E. Lee was one of them.

Indeed, he not only endured the excruciating regimen, he thrived on it, quickly finding a comfortable stride and never losing it. While every other cadet earned from a few to an expellable number of demerits for offenses such as tardiness to class, unpolished buttons, disrespecting superiors, being absent without permission, drinking, womanizing, and fighting, Robert E. Lee was and still is the only cadet to have graduated from the United States Military Academy without a single demerit. And he seems to have accomplished that feat without the attitude of superiority that so often accompanies such achievement.

Lee rose to become the revered Adjutant of the Corps of Cadets, graduated second in his class, and earned the respectful

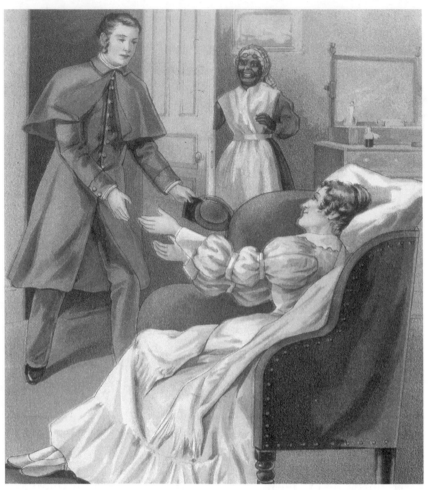

After spending five long years at West Point Military Academy, Lee hurries home to his ill mother. From a young age, Lee ran his mother's household, taking care of her and his siblings.

sobriquet the "Marble Model" or the "Marble Man" for his statuelike perfection. His high standing also earned him an assignment as a second lieutenant in the then prestigious U.S. Army Corps of Engineers. And so Lieutenant Robert E. Lee was an army officer at last, though his potential was far from being realized.

Professional Boredom, Marital Bliss, and Agony Over the Slaves

After several weeks of unsuccessfully attempting to nurse his cherished mother back to health, he lost her and sought solace in the monotonous duties of his first assignment: building a coastal defense fort near Savannah, Georgia, later named Fort Pulaski. Two lonely years later, he married the only girl he had ever loved. She was Mary Custis, the great-granddaughter of Martha Washington. She and her young husband teased each other playfully, and she never lost her profound influence over Robert's actions and opinions.

Upon marrying Mary, he inherited the Custis's Arlington plantation overlooking the city of Washington, a plantation with waving fields, fertile orchards, a pillared mansion, and 250 slaves. Robert took over the active management of Arlington and wasted no time in devising a long-range plan for the emancipation of the slaves who had come into his possession.

He had always viewed slavery uncomfortably in spite of growing up with a few beloved household servants. But he knew that slavery could never be peacefully abolished in one sudden sweep. Where would the ex-slaves go? What would they do? And how could the slave owners be compensated for their loss? His instincts told him that the blacks would be better off back in Africa, perhaps in Liberia where previously freed slaves had reestablished their own country. Or maybe the Caribbean Islands could offer a refuge where they could start their own nations and regain their personal integrity. In the meantime, though, his mind and efforts were, by necessity, directed away from the slavery issue and onto his duties as an army engineer.

Family and Fatherhood

After spending several years refurbishing Fortress Monroe, which guarded the entrance to the Chesapeake Bay, he found himself behind a desk in Washington. He was happy at last to be able to live at home and spend time with his beloved family, a privilege he had cherished and longed for when away, as evidenced by this letter to his wife regarding an infant son: "My sweet little boy, what would I give to see him. I am waking all night to hear his sweet little voice and if in the morning I could only feel his little arms around my neck and his dear little heart fluttering against my breast, I should be too happy." [15] Of a daughter, the enamored father wrote, "The brightest flower blooming among the honeysuckles and yellow jasmine of Arlington is my daughter, O, she is a rare one." [16] He and his wife eventually had seven children (George, Mary, William, Annie, Agnes, Robert, and Mildred) and family life offered him his most heartfelt pleasures.

"The Savior of St. Louis"

Lee grew bored with the routine paperwork in Washington and the lack of any chance for advancement there. He volunteered to help survey the boundary line separating Michigan and Ohio. Upon returning as a first lieutenant for his efforts, he put in for another field assignment. This one was highly prized by everyone in the engineer corps, and most important, would allow the chosen officer's family to accompany him. The job was in St. Louis, Missouri, where the fate of that booming frontier city literally rested in the hands of the man the army sent to its rescue. And that man was Robert E. Lee.

The Missouri River had been dumping tons of silt into the Mississippi River and islands were forming just off the thriving port of St. Louis. If the current of the two rivers could not be somehow diverted from the Illinois side of the Mississippi to the Missouri side, the docks would have to close. St. Louis would become the largest ghost town in America.

Over a three-year period during which he was continually criticized for perceived delays, Robert E. Lee planned and directed a mammoth operation, the scope of which had not been seen in the country up until that time. About his critics, he said without rancor, "They have a right to do as they wish with their own; I do not own the city. The Government has sent me here as an officer of the army to do a certain work. I shall do it." [17]

And do it he did. He filled barges with boulders, positioned them with mathematical precision, and sank them attached by chains beneath the surface, forming an underwater "dam" that forced the currents back over to the St. Louis side. The effect was immediate and desired. The river washed away the silt islands, bore a new channel alongside the docks, and silenced his critics. His feat also earned him the rank of captain and allowed him to associate with some of the army's leaders.

In one such opportunity, he met commander in chief of the army Winfield Scott, who asked Lee to serve with him on a board examining prospective West Point graduates. Captain Lee naturally accepted and performed his duties so admirably that General Scott remarked that he might call on him again.

Baptism and Springboard

That call came in 1846 at the beginning of the Mexican War. Lee had not approved of this land-grabbing venture (Texas, New Mexico, Arizona, California, and other Southwestern areas were among the prizes then belonging to Mexico). He wrote his wife at the outset of hostilities,

> I never could see the advantage to be gained by sending [Americans into Mexican territory] unless it was to invite

Hundreds of American troops land on the shores of Vera Cruz, Mexico, in 1846, during the Mexican-American War. Although Lee did not approve of U.S. aims in the war, he served with distinction as the third highest-ranking engineer officer.

the Mexicans to attack on account of the feebleness of our force and thus bring on the war that we had not the frankness or manliness at once to declare.[18]

Regardless, Lee wanted in on any promised action that might lead to the combat for which he had so long trained.

At Vera Cruz, Mexico, General Scott sent for Lee to serve on his general staff as the third highest-ranking engineer officer. It represented an honor and an opportunity beyond the dreams of any professional soldier. And he determined to take full advantage of it. He scouted behind enemy lines in search of their positions and hid artillery batteries from Mexican fire while enabling them to deliver their own maximum firepower. Vera Cruz fell in March 1846.

The narrow pass at Cerro Gordo on the road to Mexico City presented a tougher problem to Scott's army. High hills flanked either side of the twisting road snaking beneath them and the Mexicans had forbiddingly bristled their crests with artillery and riflemen. The situation looked bleak for the Americans who could see no other option but a bloody frontal assault. Robert E. Lee had a suggestion, though, and General Scott's interest was piqued. The captain volunteered to secretly swing a battery of artillery behind the Mexican positions, hack a road out of the nearly impenetrable chaparral and mesquite, and haul the big guns up the rear guard hills by rope, sweat, muscle, and pulley.

At one point while Lee scouted alone, ahead of the party, a squad of Mexican soldiers nearly spotted him at a water hole. All that Lee could do was roll himself under a hollow log and remain motionless. Some of the Mexicans even sat down on the log, unaware that an American soldier was nearly being crushed beneath them. Fighting every urge to squirm, scratch, or cough, Lee hid until the Mexicans finally left several hours later.

Once Lee had made his way back to the guns and properly positioned them, he gave the signal for the Americans in front to attack while his artillery opened up from the rear. The cross fire threw the Mexicans into a confusion that soon led to panic and they retreated, leaving the Americans in possession of the field once again. It was April 1847; for Captain Lee's courage, General Scott promoted him to major. Similar gallantry at the gates of Mexico City helped win the final battle of the Mexican War and earned Lee even greater accolades from the top general in the army.

In his official reports, Winfield Scott wrote that the duties Lee performed were "the greatest feats of physical and moral courage performed by any individual, in my knowledge, pending the campaign. He was the very best soldier in the field." [19] With such commendations, Major Lee was now, in the eyes of his peers, undoubtedly destined for some martial greatness.

The Lull Before the Storm

Lee's greatness did not come quickly, however; at least not in the manner he might have wished. The War Department could find no more apt use for "the Hero of Cerro Gordo" than to have him inspect coastal fortifications from New England to the Gulf of Mexico. That mundane task completed, they stationed him in Baltimore where he could put his engineering skills to use bolstering the harbor defenses.

General Winfield Scott again came to Lee's aid and landed him the plum assignment as superintendent at West Point. He chose, during his three-year tenure, not to make any sweeping changes, but he did tighten discipline while simultaneously expressing a previously unheard-of compassion for the cadets (one of whom was his oldest son). In spite of considerable criticism from the military establishment, Commandant Lee opened his office and his home to any cadet with a problem, including a boy who was upset at being called "Beauty" in mockery of his actual homeliness. That boy was J. E. B. "Jeb" Stuart, who would later rise to become the top Confederate cavalry commander.

The promise of war with the Indians in Texas prompted General Scott to send Lee there as second in command of a cavalry regiment. Lee expressed considerable hesitation regarding the transfer for he knew it would mean a lengthy period away from his bedridden, arthritic wife, whom he had been nursing with the same self-denying devotion that he had shown his mother. But he went to the Southwest anyway with high hopes for a combat command.

However, Texas proved to be no more adventuresome than any of his administrative jobs. He spent most of his time traveling through the sultry region to sit on court-martial panels. When he received word that his father-in-law had died and his wife needed his care more than ever, he sought and received a leave of absence and rushed back to Arlington.

Martyrs and Madmen

He was still there in 1859 when the army called him back to active duty for the express purpose of putting down an attempted takeover of the federal arsenal in Harpers Ferry, Virginia (now West Virginia), led by John Brown. Without time for ethical or moral reflection regarding the slavery issue, Lee and his lieutenant, J. E. B. "Beauty" Stuart, immediately obeyed their orders and attacked Brown with a small contingent of U.S. Marines. They bashed down the doors of the arsenal firehouse that was serving as the Brown faction's fortress and quelled the resistance with surprisingly little loss of life, although the state of Virginia subsequently tried and hanged John Brown for treason.

Radical abolitionist John Brown was viewed as both martyr and madman.

While the extreme abolitionists in the North quickly lionized Brown as a martyr and the secessionists in the South equally vilified him, Lee, always the moderate, still did not believe that this isolated incident

29

rendered a civil war inevitable. Surely, he thought, cooler heads in both the North and the South could see the Brown uprising in the same way he did: "an inconsequential plan that was nothing more than the attempt of a fanatic or madman." [20] This statement proved to be a rare glitch in Colonel Lee's usually astute reasoning, one that would prove him woefully wrong.

Two years later when war did come, Lee returned to Arlington from his post in Texas and regretfully resigned from the U.S. Army. He had always said that he would never raise his sword against his native Virginia, his country, and now Virginia beckoned him to go South and ply his talents there. Confederate president Jefferson Davis and every citizen of Virginia had heard of Robert E. Lee, the hero of the Mexican War and, more recently, the captor of John Brown. It was understandable that they would count on great and immediate triumphs from the Marble Man.

Granny Lee

But those triumphs did not come, certainly not with any immediacy. In August and September of 1861, then General Lee led a Confederate army into the rugged mountains of western Virginia (now West Virginia) in what came to be called the Cheat Mountain campaign. He was to expel the considerable Union forces from the area and secure the western counties of Virginia for the Confederacy. But everything that could have gone wrong did.

The laurel-thicketed mountainsides and narrow, twisting ravines often reduced marching columns to single files, quadrupling the time it took to maneuver troops. Rain fell in cascading sheets that could nearly be parted by hand. The mud sank horses to their knees and sucked the boots off the men's feet. Wild neighing and exasperated cursing perforated the sloshing, sluicing, and splashing sounds of a near-continual cloudburst.

Gunpowder became soaked, rations went soggy, and wet, woolen uniforms chafed skin raw. When the weather cleared enough, General Lee sent couriers on horseback to transmit his orders to three other Confederate detachments supposedly under his command. He then discovered that his subordinates were willfully disobeying him due to petty resentments over who should be outranking whom.

Without engaging the Unionists in any significant way, Lee finally returned to Richmond and endured scathing attacks by all the newspapers. The citizenry read the articles and exaggerated them as only gossips can, until the general who had gone to western Virginia as the Marble Man had returned with two new nicknames: Granny Lee and Evacuation Lee. With as much bitterness as his honor would allow, General Lee wrote his wife, "I know the newspaper editors can regulate matters satisfactorily to themselves on paper. I wish they could do so in the field."[21]

One More Humiliation

Jefferson Davis still had faith in Lee's potential and could appreciate the problems that had stymied him in the gnarled mountains of western Virginia. Certain of Lee's abilities as an engineer, Davis next placed him in charge of strengthening the coastal defenses throughout South Carolina, Georgia, and Florida. The digging and shoveling was arduous and boring in the extreme, especially for the eager boys and young men who had volunteered to grapple hand to hand with the evil invaders. Lee wrote his son Custis,

> Our defenses are growing stronger, but progress slowly. The volunteers dislike work, and there is much sickness among them besides. Guns are required, ammunition and more men. Still, on the whole, if the enemy does not approach in overwhelming numbers, we ought to hold our ground.[22]

Confederate president Jefferson Davis (pictured) had faith in Lee's abilities, though others had doubts about his ability to lead.

Due to either providence as Lee suspected or incompetence on the part of the Union generals, no such attack came. And finally, when the task was more or less completed, Davis sent for Lee. The president had a new assignment for him, though it was still not the combat command in the field that he so wanted.

Just when Union general George McClellan began his Peninsular campaign from the Atlantic inland to Richmond, Jefferson Davis named Lee "the commander under the direction of the President for coordinating military operations of the Confederacy."[23] However, Lee referred to the promotion as "the forlorn hope, one worse than western Virginia"[24] because he had not yet established his credibility with the officers whose military operations he was supposed to coordinate. His first stint as military advisor to Davis had kept him from taking part in the first victory over the Yankees at Manassas and his efforts in western Virginia had done nothing to improve his standing with the field commanders presumably beneath him. Many of them refused to obey his directives and some would not communicate with him at all. Those who did opposed his defensive tactics (digging in just outside Richmond and waiting for the Unionists to attempt costly frontal assaults). Lee thus received yet another derogatory moniker, the King of Spades, and was once again the butt of every joke in the state.

The Joke Stops Here

By June 1862, McClellan was pushing the Confederates under General Joseph E. Johnston farther and farther back. There was talk at a meeting of presidential advisors about evacuating Richmond and turning it over to the advancing Unionist troops. Trem-

Union general George McClellan's Peninsular campaign almost broke the forces of the South, but Lee was able to force McClellan's troops into retreat.

Union troops gather in Fair Oaks, Virginia, in June 1862. Although the Union had a great advantage in numbers over Lee's troops, the cautious McClellan often refused to engage his soldiers in the numbers required to achieve a decisive victory.

bling, and shedding the only public tears that anyone had ever seen, Robert E. Lee temporarily lost his fabled control and implored the high-ranking gathering in a loud, shaking voice, "But . . . but Richmond must be defended!"[25] The stunned room went silent; searching glances were exchanged. And, in the end, Lee had his way.

By then, Johnston's Confederates had already fallen back to the huge earthworks protecting east Richmond (which the Southerners were suddenly glad the King of Spades had erected). A huge, chaotic battle erupted near there at a thicketed crossroads known variously as Fair Oaks or Seven Pines. The casualties grew rapidly; one of them was General Johnston himself, with grotesque injuries to his chest and shoulder. When Jefferson Davis promoted Robert E. Lee to replace him, the convalescing Johnston said of his old friend and West Point classmate,

> The shot that struck me down is the very best for the Southern cause yet . . . and now the Confederate government has one who can accomplish what I never could have done—the concentration of our armies for the defense of the capital of the Confederacy.[26]

Displaying a rediscovered bravado, Lee left a skeleton force to man the earthworks in front of Richmond, betting that the cautious George McClellan would not dare attack it. He then surreptitiously (that is, secretly) sent the bulk of his army around to his left flank (the Unionist's right flank). In the bloodiest week yet of the Civil War, Lee attacked daily at Mechanicsville, Beaver Dam Creek, Gaines' Mill, Frayser's Farm, White Oak Swamp, and Malvern Hill. In every battle, the Confederates lost more men than did the Unionists but Union general McClellan retreated after each, unwilling to risk anything more in the face of this Lee fellow who seemed willing to risk everything.

The Seven Days' Battle, as it came to be called, pushed the Yankees miles away from Richmond and they did not chance another attack against the reckless Rebels. The Southern newspapers now exalted General Lee as "the Savior of Richmond" but Lee did not celebrate. Following a pattern that would dog him throughout the war, he slipped into a period of remorse over what the victory had cost in suffering to his men.

Lee Turns the Tables

Once he had rested and refit his troops, General Lee again counted on George McClellan's sluggishness. He sent Thomas J. "Stonewall" Jackson north with his seventeen-thousand-man division to meet yet another Union army of fifty thousand men under the command of General John Pope that was descending overland toward Richmond. Even Lee, who harbored so little personal ill will against his adversaries, openly reviled this pompous braggart.

And with good reason. Pope had goaded his Unionists,

> Let us understand each other. I have come to you from the West, where we have always seen the backs of our enemies; from an army whose business it has been to seek the adversary and to beat him when found; whose policy has been attack and not defense.[27]

Even more infuriating to Lee was Pope's promise to live off the Southern civilians and expose any resisters to "the extreme rigors of military law."[28] For perhaps the first and only time of the war, Robert E. Lee had a personal vendetta to satisfy against a man. And he lost no time in its satisfaction, smashing Pope's forces at the Second Battle of Manassas in August 1862.

General Lee's star had risen at last. His fame reached many continents. He had, in three months' time, cleared the enemy from around his own capital and was now glowering down on the enemy at Washington. All but mountainous western Virginia was free of invaders and it was appearing more and more as if the citizens did not want to be freed of them. The circumstances had never looked better for him to launch an invasion of his own, one, perhaps, so consequential as to gain European aid and recognition and thereby achieve Southern independence once and for all.

The Bold Gamble

With the indecisive George McClellan once again commanding from Washington, Lee wasted no time crossing the Potomac River into Union-held Maryland and setting up camp near Frederick. He issued a friendly invitation for all Marylanders to rise up against what he called the wrongs and outrages of the United States but no such uprising resulted. In spite of that, he gambled on what President Lincoln himself called McClellan's case of the slows and divided his vastly outnumbered army into four smaller commands, each with its distinct mission in his overall plan. Though risky and opposed by most of his subordinates, the strategy had every chance of leading to a victorious invasion of the North. There was just one problem.

A copy of the orders dividing his army fell into the hands of McClellan. Lee suddenly found his typically turtle-paced adversary invigorated and about to plow into the middle of his forces and beat them in detail. Never one to panic, Lee called upon his separated forces to reunite at a centrally located village known as Sharpsburg on bluffs overlooking the west side of Antietam Creek. Lee's Army of Northern Virginia began dribbling into Sharpsburg on September 15 and 16. If McClellan had attacked on either of those days, the Civil War might have ended right then and there. But, true to his form, the Yankee waited until September 17 and even then he outmatched Lee two-to-one.

In twelve solid hours of battle, first in Miller's Cornfield, then the Bloody Lane, Burnside's Bridge, and finally Sharpsburg Ridge, the Yankees bent but they could not break the Rebel lines. And in a stroke of what Lee could only believe was "God's will," A. P. Hill's last-minute reinforcements crashed into the Union flank and sent them reeling back to the same positions from which they had started the day.

It had been the bloodiest single day in American history and neither side could call it more than a draw. But Robert E. Lee refused to fall back, willing to take on McClellan again the next day. When it became evident that the Union general was not game, Lee retired to Virginia. His attempted invasion of the North had been turned back but there would be another, he knew, in its own time. For now, however, he had to look to his primary responsibility: defending his home, his country, his beloved Virginia.

Highs and Lows

Robert E. Lee's moods varied in the weeks and months following the horrors of Antietam. McClellan could have easily pursued and beaten the exhausted Confederates but he did not and, as a result, he lost his job to Ambrose Burnside. Lee took the opportunity to remark, "I fear they may continue to make these changes until they find someone whom I don't understand." [29] Burnside was not to be that someone.

Lee oversees the progress of the battle at Fredericksburg on December 13, 1862. Lee would win a decisive victory in the battle, though success was mingled with sadness when he learned that his twenty-three-year-old daughter, Annie, had died.

In the snow of December 13, 1862, Lee's well-dug-in army hurled back wave after wave of Union soldiers at Fredericksburg, Virginia. Lee revealed something of his deeper, darker self when, looking over the aftermath of the fighting, he muttered, "It is well that war is so terrible or we should grow too fond of it." [30]

The winter respite that followed the lopsided victory should have enthused Lee but it did not. His precious twenty-three-year-old daughter, Annie, had died of typhoid fever in October. After a few weeks of unexpressed grief, he broke down in a letter and confessed, "when I think of her in the quiet hours of the night, when there is nothing to lighten the full weight of my grief, I feel as if I should be overwhelmed." [31] His personal tragedy deepened when his newborn granddaughter died without having been baptized.

However, his building frustration did not end with his immediate family. The Confederate government was not properly supporting his army, which was badly in need of food, clothing, shoes, ammunition, and replacements, causing him to write in an uncharacteristic tirade,

> What has our Congress done to meet the exigency, I should say extremity, in which we are placed? Cannot they do something for us? The only place I am to be found is in camp, and I am so cross that I am not worth seeing anywhere. Congress seem to be laboring to pass laws to get easy places for some favorite or constituent or to get others out of active service. I shall be very much obliged to them if they will pass a law relieving me from all duty and legislating someone in my place better able to do it. [32]

A Sensitive Heart Begins to Break

Robert E. Lee had long opposed slavery and held his personal servants in extremely high regard. Although he knew his actions would not change the general sentiment regarding slavery in the South, he did, during the winter of 1862–1863, legally "manumit, emancipate, and forever set free" [33] all of his slaves. To ensure that none in temporary service to other masters would be overlooked, he personally transcribed 170 names of slaves he wanted freed. He also immediately began paying his personal servant, Perry, and his cook, George, $8.20 per month with hopes that "they lay up [save] something for themselves," [34] presumably because now there would be no one to care for them in their old age.

In spite of the satisfaction he felt in finally freeing his slaves, General Lee slipped slowly into a vague malaise during the winter of 1862–1863. Pains pierced his chest and aches entwined his

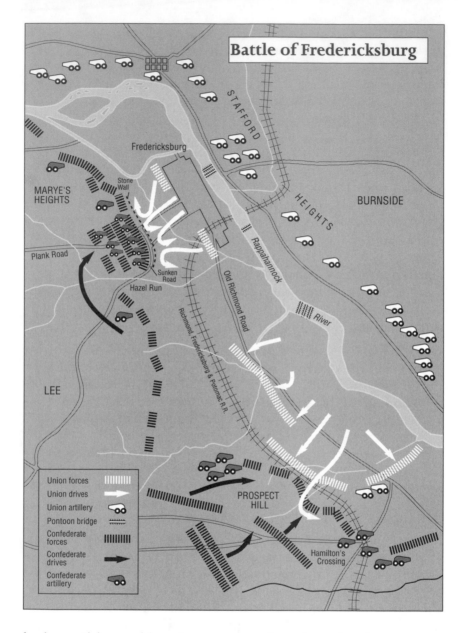

Battle of Fredericksburg

STAFFORD

HEIGHTS

BURNSIDE

Fredericksburg

Stone Wall

MARYE'S HEIGHTS

Plank Road

Sunken Road

Hazel Run

Rappahannock

Old Richmond Road

Richmond, Fredericksburg & Potomac R.R.

River

LEE

PROSPECT HILL

Hamilton's Crossing

Union forces
Union drives
Union artillery
Pontoon bridge
Confederate forces
Confederate drives
Confederate artillery

body until he could no longer conceal or deny that he was seriously ill. This Marble Man who rarely complained admitted to

> a good deal of pain in my chest, back, and arms . . . that comes on in paroxysms and are quite sharp . . . my pulse rate is still about 90. . . . I feel pins and am remarkably unsteady. . . . I am feeble and worthless and can do but little. . . . I feel oppressed by what I have to undergo for the first time in my life.[35]

Today, doctors would probably discuss the general's ailments in terms such as angina pectoris or inflammation of the pericardium. They might even diagnose a mild cardiac arrest, serious enough to eventually cause the apoplexy (stroke) that killed him and most definitely serious enough to reduce his capabilities as a commanding field officer during the remaining campaigns of the War Between the States.

But, apparently, ill health did not hamper him in the next campaign at Chancellorsville. For there, assisted by a flanking maneuver brilliantly executed by Stonewall Jackson, Lee again flushed the

Lee is greeted enthusiastically by his troops after their hard won victory at Chancellorsville, Virginia. Lee won the campaign, but lost Stonewall Jackson, who died after being accidentally shot by his own troops.

Yankees from Virginia. Jackson died during that victory as a result of "friendly fire," that is, fire mistakenly aimed at one's own forces. With Jackson's loss, both the figurative and literal pains grew in Lee's heart as he made plans for his second invasion of the North.

The Heart and the Marble Crack Further

Ignoring intermittent pains in his chest, General Lee took advantage of the summer season and the momentum his victorious army had built up by invading Pennsylvania. The Army of Northern Virginia had never been larger, and its string of victories never longer. He was confident in his men (perhaps a little too much so) and just as confident in the Union army's continuing lack of sound leadership.

The two huge forces collided on the farmlands and bouldered hillsides near Gettysburg, Pennsylvania, and battled for two horrific days. Strangely (to those unaware of his poor health), Lee seemed listless and unwilling to consider reasonable advice from trusted generals about alternative strategies. Granted, he was operating without the eyes and ears of the army. General J. E. B. Stuart had his cavalry on a raid and was absent from his reconnaissance duties. But beyond that, Lee appeared tired and less focused than such frustrations would have warranted in the past.

Lee was uncharacteristically stubborn in his decisions during the battle at Gettysburg, Pennsylvania. His lack of insight on these two days led him to order his troops to charge Union troops in a hopelessly ill-fated maneuver that came to be known as Pickett's Charge. The charge resulted in the deaths of 12,000 men—men whom the South could not replace.

Once he decided upon a strategy, no one seemed able to budge him from it, even though most could see its folly. And on the third day of battle, July 3, 1863, he committed his greatest folly as a battlefield commander. He ordered Pickett's Charge, where twelve thousand brave, dutiful Southern soldiers marched and then charged across an open, mile-wide, uphill grade while being torn to pieces by Union guns and rifles. Of course, the attack failed and, accepting responsibility for the bloody debacle, Lee rode among the returning survivors, apologizing to them over and over, "You men have done all that men could do: the fault is entirely my own." [36]

An officer present when Lee finally returned to his headquarters that night was shocked at the once invincible general's appearance. He recalled:

> General Lee was almost too tired to dismount. The effort betrayed so much physical exhaustion that I hurriedly rose and stepped forward to assist him, but before I reached his side he had succeeded in alighting and threw his arm across the saddle to rest, and fixing his eyes upon the ground leaned in silence and almost motionless upon his equally weary horse, the two forming a striking group. The moon shone full upon his massive features and revealed an expression of sadness that I had never before seen on his face. The General remained silent for a time and then said in a loud voice, "Too bad! *Too bad!* OH, TOO BAD!" [37]

Too bad, indeed. For the defeat at Gettysburg portended the gradual deaths of both General Lee and the Confederacy itself. It would only be a matter of time before the sequence of those deaths would play itself out.

The Declining Years

Gettysburg (and compounding losses throughout the South) destroyed any real hope for a free and independent Confederate States of America. But honor, pride, cultural heritage, and stubbornness caused thousands upon thousands of Rebel soldiers to maintain their arms. Chief among them was Robert Edward Lee. Even when the jackhammering General Ulysses S. Grant took over the Union armies and began trading the Confederates death for death (a grisly statistical strategy that only the outnumbering Unionists could win), Lee still would not quit. Understandably, more and more of his men did, though, deserting to seek food, warmth, shelter, and safety among their families. But Lee and his faithful few held on, more from a sense of duty than any real hope of preventing the South's inevitable demise.

Yet even Lee's resolve was weakening. He tried to resign once, citing, among other reasons, "the growing failure of my bodily strength, my [heart] attack of last Spring, and my lessened capability of exertion" [38] only to have Jefferson Davis refuse the request. At increasingly bloody battles during 1864 such as the Wilderness and Spotsylvania, he intentionally and rashly exposed himself to intense fire as if seeking an honorable end to his suffering. A general mood of emotional depression was at least partially clouding his mental processes. Lee was seen grieving J. E. B. Stuart's death as if overcome by waves of physical weakness. He broke down without pretense and sobbed at the loss of A. P. Hill, muttering, "He is now at rest and we who are left are the ones to suffer." [39]

General Lee managed to stiffen his will, however, and he spent the last few gasps of the Army of Northern Virginia defending a long network of trenches that protected Petersburg and, hence, Richmond from final envelopment. He kept the remnants of the Confederate army breathing and the ponderous Union army at bay for ten months (far longer than Lincoln and Grant expected). But in April 1865, a tidal wave of Yankees washed General Lee and his survivors out into the Virginia countryside to a village called Appomattox Court House. There Lee left what were, perhaps, the most indelible glimpses of his character.

The Ordeal of Surrender

For a man who had never given up any challenge he had undertaken, early April 1865 required more stamina, conviction, and emotional fortitude than any other time in his life. While still at Petersburg, he had probed General Grant with a suggestion that they meet, "desiring to leave nothing untried which may put an end to the calamities of war" [40] but Grant replied that only President Lincoln could conduct such talks. Grant apparently changed his mind a month later and proposed a meeting near Appomattox Court House. After a few clarifications, field maneuvers, and counterproposals (during which Lee postured his band of ragged soldiers for a last flush of gallant defiance), he accepted a meeting set for the morning of April 9 at the private residence of one Wilmer McClean.

General Lee rode in with a small entourage, wearing his finest dress uniform and ceremonial sword. He had not been on a horse

General Robert E. Lee surrendered to Union general Ulysses S. Grant on April 9, 1865, at Appomattox.

for several weeks by then. He preferred the relative comfort of an ambulance wagon due to the painful jostling horseback riding caused his chest cavity. He took a seat inside the comfortably appointed parlor and waited thirty minutes for Grant to appear. The cigar-chomping Unionist finally shuffled in dressed in rough garb and splattered with mud. The two spoke amicably of their Mexican War associations. Lee sensed that Grant remembered him but he had trouble placing Grant, though, gentleman that he was, he did not say so.

When Lee suggested that they get down to the matter at hand, General Grant, surrounded by a dozen or so of his subordinates, penned the generous terms of surrender. Lee, sitting erect and impassively while his two aides stood, read over the document with a sense of relief and asked to make a few minor changes. Grant conceded. After twenty minutes, the ceremony ended as did, for all practical purposes, the Civil War. Lee concealed his pain, mounted up, and rode away, tipping his hat to General Grant and the awed crowd of Yankees who had gathered outside. When he was gone, cheers erupted, which Grant respectfully silenced.

The Man Fades Away

Robert E. Lee did not like to give speeches and he was not a particularly eloquent writer. He did love his troops, though, more than any words could express. He released the following farewell to be shared with every soldier who had lasted with him until the end:

After four years of arduous service, marked by unsurpassed courage and fortitude, the Army of Northern Virginia has been compelled to yield to overwhelming numbers and resources.

I need not tell the brave survivors of so many hard fought battles, who have remained steadfast to the last, that I have consented to the result from no distrust of them.

The "Marble Model" resigned from the army shortly after his surrender to General Grant in 1865. Lee lived the last five years of his life quietly in Lexington, Virginia, and died in 1870.

But feeling that valor and devotion could accomplish nothing that would compensate for the loss that must have attended the continuance of the contest, I determined to avoid the useless sacrifice of those whose past services have endeared them to their countrymen.

By the terms of the agreement officers and men can return to their homes and remain until exchanged. You will take with you the satisfaction that proceeds from the consciousness of duty faithfully performed, and I earnestly pray that a Merciful God will extend to you His blessing and protection.

With our increasing admiration of your constancy and devotion to your country, and a grateful remembrance of your kind and generous considerations for myself, I bid you all an affectionate farewell.[41]

And with that, Robert Edward Lee resigned from the army and sought obscurity as the president of a tiny college by the name of Washington College in the tiny town of Lexington, in the backwaters of Virginia, shunning all further efforts to venerate and glorify him. He died five years later from the ailments that had plagued him since Fredericksburg. However, he failed in those fading years to achieve the humble obscurity he had sought for so long. It is ironic that, in death, his legend grew to such huge proportions that, in a way, he was finally forgotten. At least the facts of his flesh-and-blood life as he had actually lived it—with its fears, frustrations, mistakes, and shortcomings—slipped from general awareness. And in its place arose the marble monument known today as Robert E. Lee.

CHAPTER 3

Thomas J. "Stonewall" Jackson: The Brilliant Fool

Brigadier General Thomas Jonathan Jackson sat bolt upright in his saddle, scanning the sulfur-smoked hilltop before him. Holding a handkerchief to his wounded left ring finger, he ordered his one thousand men to lie down in the tall, golden grass behind him to avoid stray bullets like the one that had nicked him. This battle had been distantly crackling all around him since dawn at Manassas Junction in Virginia and now, at noon on July 21, 1861, it was about to boil over his frightened troops.

Jackson had driven his Virginians hard to place them strategically on Henry House Hill behind the Confederates' first line of defense, and he had done so with only minutes to spare. For just as he had drawn his infantry and artillery into battle formation, the first Rebel line crumbled before an overwhelming Union advance and its remnants began retreating to the rear.

Troops on a bridge during the battle of Manassas. Led by General Stonewall Jackson, the battle resulted in one of the first major victories for the South.

"Steady, men," the drably uniformed Jackson monotoned as he sauntered up and down the line on his undersized mount. "Steady . . . steady. . . ." But his sweating soldiers appeared far from assured.

General Barnard Bee, in a frantic attempt to rally the shattered ranks, galloped up to Jackson through the intensifying explosions and zipping bullets. Ducking down nervously, he exclaimed, "General! They are beating us back! What shall we do?" His blue eyes suddenly alive with fire, Jackson replied, "Sir, we will give them the bayonet." [42]

Inspired by that resolution, General Bee whipped his horse to a frenzy and charged out among his disintegrated ranks shouting, "There stands Jackson like a stone wall! Rally behind the Virginians! There stands Jackson like a stone wall! Rally! Rally!" [43]

And though a Yankee bullet felled Bee in the next instant, his tattered men did rally and file into Jackson's line. The battle

General Thomas Jackson's bravery at the battle of Manassas earned him the nickname "Stonewall." Jackson became known for his calmness during times of calamity.

was not yet over and it certainly was not yet won, but a hero was on the verge of emerging, assuming, of course, that "Stonewall" could live up to his new name. And that would not be easy.

Over the next three hours, Union troops charged across Henry House Hill, screaming, shooting, killing, and dying. And through it all Jackson's stone wall held. Union artillery fired within three hundred yards of the Confederates and blasted at the human wall but breathless Southern reinforcements kept arriving just in time to plug the gaps and mount sporadic countercharges of their own. During the seesawing battle, Jackson remained calmly mounted, reassuring his men with his stolid equanimity. Bullets tore through his clothing, wounded his horse, and injured men all around him but he held his brigade intact until the optimum moment for a full-scale attack arrived.

With Confederate cavalry and fresh infantry finally threatening the Union flanks, General Jackson passed on the long-awaited order to his stone-wall brigade anchoring the center, "Charge, men! Charge! Give them the bayonet!" [44] And at last, the tide began to turn in favor of the Southerners.

"The charge of Jackson's men was terrific," wrote one who witnessed it. "The enemy were swept before them like chaff before a whirlwind." [45] Jackson himself referred to that part of the fight as "the hardest that I have ever been in." [46] The battle and the complete rout that followed made the First Battle of Manassas (or Bull Run) the worst Union humiliation of the entire war and one of the greatest of all Southern victories. It also gave birth to the legend of Stonewall Jackson.

An Odd Sort of Legend

Arguably, Stonewall Jackson's most profound effect on history, his greatest legacy, lies not in what he did but in who he was, not in his remarkable achievements but in the fact that they could have been achieved at all by a man referred to most of his life as "Old Tom Fool." For no Confederate general embodied more oddities and contradictions than did Thomas Jonathan Jackson. And few ever exhibited any less promise of greatness at the outset of the Civil War.

One eminent historian wrote, "In February, 1861, few had appraised Jackson as an able soldier. Some of his officers and many of his troops thought him eccentric, if not insane." Even his second in command subscribed to this opinion, reporting to a superior, "Did it ever occur to you that General Jackson is crazy? I tell you, Sir, he is as crazy as a March hare. I tell you, he is crazy!" [47] And it is little wonder that he and so many others thought so.

Jackson was born in 1824 and orphaned five years later when both his parents died of illness. Since his childhood near Weston in western Virginia (now West Virginia), Thomas Jackson had sought order from the chaos of family upheaval. He developed and practiced a set of rigid, moralist rules that he penned in a notebook and studied regularly. The maxims themselves, such as "tell the truth," "do what you set out to do," and "you may be whatever you resolve to be," were laudable but the extremism he brought to bear on their execution bordered on the fanatical.

He was, in spite of his rigidity, a dreamy boy, often seen walking along the dusty roads nearly at attention, yet leaning forward as if into a gale-force wind. And always his thoughts appeared to be on some far-off, lonely place. The bachelor uncles who had taken him in kidded him mercilessly but lovingly for his serious and eccentric nature. The uncles themselves were prone to loud laughter and ribald joking. But one uncle, Cummins Jackson, took a particular liking to the odd boy and always attempted to make him feel at home with the rowdy houseful of men.

A Yearning for Something More

Young Thomas went to school as much as the other farm boys in the hill country, three winter months per year between harvesting and planting times. There he picked up the basics of reading, writing, and ciphering (arithmetic). He never did develop an ease for reading, however, which caused him difficulties with all of his subjects.

Thomas's father, who had died when the boy was only five, had been a lawyer in the muddy but bustling frontier town of Clarksburg. He did not achieve great success, though, because he could not refuse a loan to a friend in need, and it seems he had many needy friends. His example and that of Thomas's uncommonly well educated mother were enough, however, to plant within the boy the vague dream of becoming an educated man himself.

In spite of his academic mediocrity, Thomas's work habits made him stand out as a boy who might someday amount to something, a preacher, some thought, or perhaps a schoolmaster if not a lawyer. He put in long and hard hours every day on the farm, never complaining or shirking his chores. As an early teen, he managed his Uncle Cummins's slave crews, overseeing the cutting and transport of timber from the rugged hillsides to their sawmill along the West Fork River. He also earned money as a jockey in local horse races, though he never looked graceful on the back of a mount.

Deep down, however, he knew he could not be happy as a farmer. His Uncle Cummins, rather than attempting to hang on to him for his valuable contributions to the farm, did all he could to arrange for some sort of higher schooling, at least an apprenticeship with a local tradesman. But young Jackson wanted college and, since he knew that his uncle had no money for that, he chose another option: the United States Military Academy at West Point, New York. There, Tom had heard, a young man could receive a first-rate education without cost and graduate as both an officer and a gentleman.

A Chance and a Second Chance

There was a problem, however. Three other boys from Weston wanted to go to the academy in 1842. The tiny congressional district in which the town was located could send only one. An examination would have to separate the future cadet from the boys who would be left behind, and seventeen-year-old Thomas went to work as only he could to prepare himself.

He took the test and then waited. Endless weeks passed on the farm and still no word came. Characteristically, he did not whine, he did not cry, he did not bemoan his circumstances in any way. Instead, he worked hard, said little, and smiled less. Even when the letter came informing him that another boy had won the nomination to West Point, young Jackson kept his disappointment to himself.

He buried himself in his everyday routine, feeding cattle, tending the grist mill, and seeing to the welfare of the many horses. It was a wet enough summer and the crops needed little attention in their sprawling, gold and green fields so there was not enough labor to fill the void where his dreams of West Point had been. Then one of the many events occurred that he would later attribute to the providential hand of God. His life changed forever. A letter arrived stating that the first candidate from Weston had quit the academy's rigorous indoctrination regimen and asking Jackson to replace him.

When his congressman asked him if he thought he could handle the difficult coursework, he sat erect on the edge of his chair and replied, "I am very ignorant but I can make it up in study. I know I have the energy and I think I have the intellect." [48]

The congressman also considered Jackson's rough-hewn appearance. He saw a young man dressed in ill-fitting homespun clothes and a hillbilly hat in his lap. All his belongings seemed to be crammed into two worn-out saddlebags. Yet, seeing the determination in the young man's eyes, the congressman gave his final approval and sent him away to the elitist school with the admonition, "Young man, if anybody at West Point insults you, give them a good beating and charge it to me." [49] Somewhat perplexed by the advice, Jackson simply replied that he was not expecting insults or planning quarrels. The congressman doubted that things would work out quite that smoothly. Events proved him right.

Struggle at the Point

The first person the uncultured Jackson met at West Point was a blue-blooded Virginia cavalier by the name of Dabney Maury. Unaware of Jackson's intensified shyness at being in such a new and intimidating environment, Dabney had approached Jackson to welcome him to West Point and remarked that Jackson "received me so coldly that I regretted my friendly overture, and rejoined my companions, rebuffed and discomfited." [50]

And that was only the beginning. The other cadets were soon teasing Jackson for his other quirks: sitting erect with toes, eyes, and head pointed meticulously to the fore (even when relaxing), mumbling to himself, and sweating profusely when called upon to recite in class. To the well-bred sons of wealth, Thomas Jackson was a strange sort of mountain man with little chance for success as an officer and a gentleman. The other boys' previous preparatory education made it that much more difficult for them to understand what a hideous torture the academic work was to him.

But Jackson would not relent. Carrying on his study habits from youth, he stayed up into the late hours of each night, reading by the fire's faint glow. He attended no parties and spent little time at recreation. He literally burned knowledge into his brain and, once it was there, tried to memorize it so it would never escape. His sister-in-law from his marriage to his first wife would later write, "He did not intuitively take in knowledge, but his mind never lost a fact or idea once committed to its keeping." [51] A former classmate would add, "No one I have ever known could so perfectly withdraw his mind from surrounding objects or influences, and so thoroughly involve his whole being in the subject under consideration." [52]

Fully uniformed and armed with rifles, West Point cadets stand in a tight circle. Jackson had to work twice as hard as his more sophisticated wealthy peers did at the academy.

While Cadet Jackson's first year at the military academy proved woeful for him both personally and academically, he did not flinch and he did not give up. Four years later, he had risen from the bottom to near the top of his class. Talk had it that if West Point had required five years of study, Thomas Jackson would have graduated first among his comrades.

And they were his comrades by that time. The other cadets had, over the years, grown to accept and even respect their coarse and ungainly classmate. Many Southerners, such as Ambrose Powell Hill, Dabney Maury, and George Pickett, would later grow to respect him as their commanding officer. Young Northerners at the Point, among them George McClellan, U. S. Grant, and Winfield Scott Hancock, would learn to respect him as their enemy. That, however, would not come to pass for another sixteen years. In the meantime, these Northern and Southern West Point graduates headed south together to fight a common foe.

First Blood

When Second Lieutenant of Artillery Thomas Jonathan Jackson returned home to Weston for the first time since leaving for West Point, he was welcomed as a hero. In his snappy, brass-buttoned uniform, he drew all the attention and accolades he had ever fantasized as a boy. The local militia had planned a military review in preparation for the impending war with Mexico, and the colonel asked him to lead one of the companies on the drill field. Jackson warned that he might not be aware of the various commands the colonel was using but the older man assured him that, with all of his military training, he could certainly figure it out as he went.

Before long the amateur colonel lost his place in the string of commands and had to stop his two raggedy companies as best as he could. In classic Jackson style, however, the young lieutenant precisely led his companies off the parade ground, onto the main road, through the town, and out into the country. When the colonel was finally able to gallop out and stop them, he implored, "My God, Tom, didn't you know enough to stop? Couldn't you tell you weren't supposed to leave the parade ground?"

Lieutenant Jackson responded simply, "Colonel, I did not receive the proper order to halt." [53]

It took several weeks of travel and the badgering of his superior officers but Lieutenant Jackson finally reached Mexico and the goal for which he had been chafing: an assignment to combat action at the front. He went into his first battle, the siege of Vera Cruz in 1846, as an artillerist with a bad case of nerves, but surprised himself to discover that he felt fine as soon as the bullets and cannonballs began to rip past him. Never again would he fear the terrible effects of weaponry during a fight, though he would often become unsettled if positioned too far in the rear.

His first taste of personal killing came in a small ambush upon his guns as he was deploying them. Though the hand-to-hand scrape proved bloody and brutal in the extreme, he would write to his sister only that, "I was detached with a few men in the vicinity of La Joya and succeeded in killing four of the enemy and taking three prisoners together with a beautiful saber and some other equipment."[54] He had already become used to the sight of mutilated bodies. Now, it seemed, he had little more reaction to doing the mutilating (or nearly becoming mutilated himself).

Heroism, Peacetime, and Boredom

Jackson's greatest triumph of the war came before the gates of Mexico City, where he exposed himself and his men to a savage fire to provide the assaulting infantry with forward artillery support. "Come on!" he cried, trying to rally his retreating crews. "There is no danger here!" Along with the shower of bullets kicking up dust around him, a Mexican cannonball smashed down near him and shot between his legs. "See, I am not hit!"

But only his commanding officer braved the lead storm to reach him, and his horse crashed down dead in the attempt. "What now, Jackson?" the commander shouted over the din.

"Help me turn this gun around and we will finish them!"[55]

And finish many of them they did, swabbing, loading, and firing the big gun over and over again until the Mexican capital fell and the United States claimed its victory. For the U.S. soldiers' efforts, Mexico ceded over half of its territory, including all or part of present-day Texas, New Mexico, Arizona, Colorado, Utah, Nevada, and California. The territories of the United States thereby increased by over one-fourth. For his bravery, Jackson was promoted to major and mentioned glowingly in his commanding officer's official reports. These words of praise were comparable to receiving a medal in an era when medals were not awarded in the U.S. Army.

Jackson remained in conquered Mexico for a while, where he learned a little Spanish, nearly became a Roman Catholic, and entertained the notion of marrying one of the pretty señoritas but, before he could take any of those leaps, the army transferred him to Florida, where he quickly became mired in the boredom of peacetime garrison duty.

American troops attack Mexico City on September 12, 1847. Jackson's persistence paid off during the storming of the city, where he refused to give up until the capital fell to U.S. troops.

There, Jackson became a devout Presbyterian and practiced his faith with characteristic single-mindedness. Refusing to undertake any type of work on Sunday, he even declined to mail a letter if he thought that postal workers might have to handle it on the Lord's day. In addition, he neither smoked, drank, nor swore and often took to task those who did. He even openly accused his commanding officer of having an adulterous affair. The inevitable conflict eventually forced him from the army.

The Eccentric Professor

Major Jackson took a job as a professor at the Virginia Military Institute and his eccentricities multiplied. He sucked regularly on lemons for his real or imagined "dyspepsia," or indigestion. (Buying the lemons was a feat in itself, for the fruit was not commonly available in the state.) He would not eat pepper because he claimed that it made his left leg ache, and he took to walking, riding, sitting, and lecturing with his left arm raised in the air so as to, as he put it, balance the organs.

Due to his difficulties reading lecture notes (and all other written matter), Professor Jackson memorized each day's lesson word for word. He sat bolt upright in a chair facing a wall and murmured the lessons over and over again until they were committed to memory. He rarely took questions from his students because, for him, answering them meant scrolling back the memorized lecture in his head and reciting it verbatim from the point of the student's inquiry. His methods frustrated several of his students to the point that they began calling him Old Tom Fool (often to his face) and had to be expelled.

One such cadet went so far as to challenge him to an old-fashioned pistol duel but friends whisked him away before he could do any serious damage to the professor. Another student nearly killed him by hurling bricks from a third-story window. Unperturbed, the professor walked on as if he were not even aware of the attack, which may well have been the case.

The Quirks Go Back to War

When the Civil War finally broke out in April 1861, Jackson felt compelled to offer his services to his beloved state of Virginia and to the Confederacy as a whole. He had, during his lifetime, owned a few house servants but he had never believed that slavery in itself was an issue worth fighting for. In fact, he considered the souls of blacks worth risking a prison term over, which happened in Lexington, Virginia, when he began teaching slaves Sunday school lessons (an offense dangerously close to teaching them the forbidden art of reading itself).

Whatever his motives for fighting, Jackson's importance to the Confederate war effort can hardly be overstated. The win at First Manassas alone (where he earned the name Stonewall) granted the Confederacy nine precious months of relative calm in which to build an army, a navy, and a government. It took the Unionists that long to reassemble their forces and risk another full-scale invasion of the South. And Jackson's maddening habit of not trusting even his highest subordinates with the details of his plans allowed him to befuddle his enemies during the spring 1862 invasion of the Shenandoah Valley in Virginia.

In a masterpiece of mobility and surprise, Stonewall defeated three separate Union armies that were converging upon him, thereby denying their much-needed use elsewhere. In fact, the name "Stonewall Jackson" had already become so fearsome in the North that President Abraham Lincoln demanded that sixty thousand Union soldiers be deployed around Washington to protect the capital from the shadowy Rebel marauder.

Following his maxim to "always surprise the enemy, if possible, and when you strike and overcome him, never give up the pursuit," [56] he pushed his "foot-cavalry" as much as thirty miles in a single day (when other generals could only coax ten), and out-marched, outmaneuvered, and outfought the Yankees up and down one hundred miles of fields, farms, mountains, and valleys. One veteran said of the feat, "Jackson gave us each forty rounds and a gum blanket [a rubberized mat for sleeping] and he drove us like hell!" [57] Satisfied that he had tied up the Unionists in the valley long enough, he slipped away and joined the fight developing around Richmond, having earned a place in history that his subsequent lackluster performance could not budge.

Quirks Grow into Qualities

After driving the Unionists from the gates of Richmond in July, the overall Confederate commander, Robert E. Lee, ordered General Jackson north to meet the threat of yet another invading Union army. Sucking on lemons and riding with his arm cocked in the air, Jackson swung widely around and behind the Yankees and destroyed their supply trains at Manassas Junction. He then took up positions behind an unfinished railroad grade near the Manassas battlefield of a year earlier and waited for the rest of the Confederate army to arrive. However, the Unionists caught up to him and launched their attack before reinforcements could make it. The fate of the Confederacy again rested upon his fabled resolve.

Early on August 29, 1862, Jackson had ridden forward and seen wave after wave of Union soldiers precisely marching on his

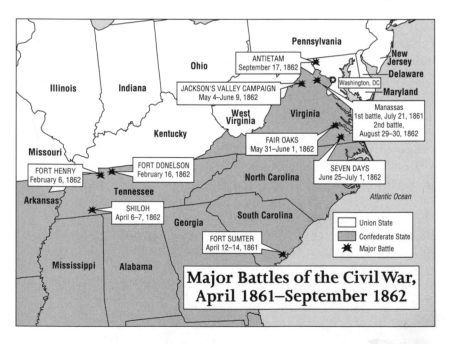

position. Several of his officers saw the same thing and were beginning to cluck like agitated hens. One of them recalled,

> Jackson rode up to the assembled group as calm as a May morning and, touching his hat in military salute, said in as soft a voice as if he were talking to a friend in ordinary conversation, "Bring up your men, gentlemen." Every officer whirled around and scurried back to their men in the woods at full gallop and from those woods shortly arose a hoarse roar like that from cages of wild beasts at the scent of blood.[58]

For half the day, thousands of Unionists slammed against the unfinished railroad embankment in a swirl of bullets, bayonets, and bombardments. In most places, Jackson's Rebels held although they suffered at least as much carnage as they inflicted. At one point, the swarming Yankees breached the left side of Jackson's line. Many of the Confederates there had run out of ammunition and were reduced to hurling rocks.

Seemingly unconcerned about any danger to himself, Jackson rode into the firestorm and inspired his men to stand like a stone wall once again. The battered men rallied and bought enough time for the rest of General Lee's army to arrive and come crashing down on the weakened Unionists, driving them back to Washington in defeat just as had happened a year earlier. The time was now right, or so Lee thought, to mount the first great invasion of the North. And Lee already had a plan in mind, one in which his oddest of generals would figure prominently.

Snatching a Draw from Certain Defeat

The resulting Maryland campaign of 1862 eventually climaxed along a little stream called Antietam near Sharpsburg, Maryland, on September 17 and exploded into the bloodiest single day in American history: the Battle of Antietam (or Sharpsburg to the Southerners). Prior to Lee taking up positions there, however, twelve thousand Yankees situated twenty miles to his rear at Harpers Ferry had to be surrounded and eliminated. The job called for a Confederate general who could move quickly and secretively, command divided forces attacking from three different sides, and sweep down fiercely upon an enemy. General Lee did not hesitate in choosing Jackson for that job.

The ardent Presbyterian carried out his mission with minimal loss of life on either side. When the Unionists saw how completely he could beat them, they laid down their arms, thirteen thousand of them, along with seventy-three artillery pieces. At that point,

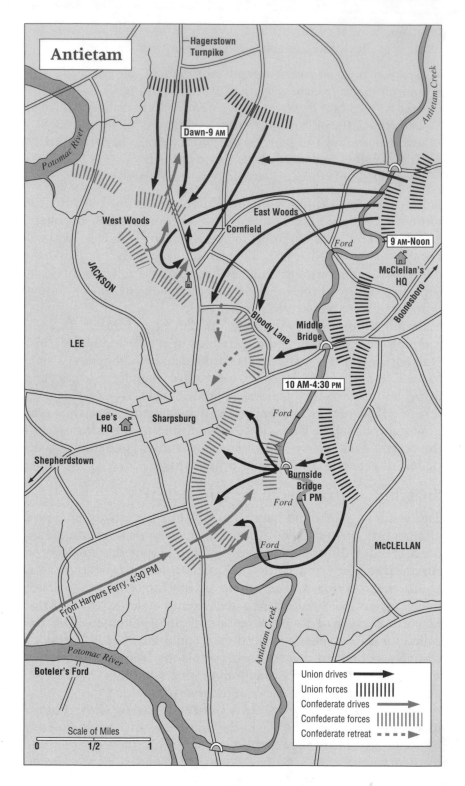

Antietam

Hagerstown Turnpike

Potomac River

Antietam Creek

Dawn-9 AM

West Woods

East Woods

Cornfield

JACKSON

Ford

9 AM-Noon

McClellan's HQ

Booneshoro

LEE

Bloody Lane

Middle Bridge

10 AM-4:30 PM

Lee's HQ

Sharpsburg

Ford

Shepherdstown

Burnside Bridge 1 PM

Ford

Ford

From Harpers Ferry, 4:30 PM

McCLELLAN

Potomac River

Antietam Creek

Boteler's Ford

Scale of Miles

0   1/2   1

Union drives

Union forces

Confederate drives

Confederate forces

Confederate retreat

58

Jackson again entered the record books for capturing more U.S soldiers at one time than in any other American engagement prior to World War II.

Even the dejected Yankees at Harpers Ferry stood in awe of him. When one prisoner criticized the general's lackluster appearance, a wiser man commented, "Boy, he is not much for looks but if he had been in command of us, we would not have been caught in this trap." [59]

And Jackson had yet more to offer in the Maryland campaign. He immediately force-marched his troops back to join Lee at Sharpsburg. Together they fought the outnumbering Federals to a bloody draw at the Battle of Antietam and prevented what could have been a total disaster for the Confederates. In typical Jackson fashion, he surveyed the aftermath of the stalemate, nearly twenty-five thousand dead and wounded bodies from both armies, and muttered, "God has been very good to us today." [60]

The Highest and Lowest Moments

In the December snows that followed outside Fredericksburg, Virginia, Lee and Jackson went on to inflict the most lopsided defeat of the war on the Unionists. They mowed down row after row of the bravest men in the North, who were being ordered up an unprotected hill by some of the most inept officers. Even charging up that slippery slope into entrenched positions, the Unionists managed to breach Jackson's line for a moment, only to be driven off like all the rest when Stonewall rallied one of his typical countercharges.

An even greater Southern victory followed in the spring at a nearby crossroads known as Chancellorsville, but it was a victory won at far too high a cost due to one man's name at the top of the casualty list. After flanking the unsuspecting Federals with one of his trademark marches and leading his men to their greatest triumph, Stonewall Jackson fell in an accidental fusillade fired at him by riflemen of his own army.

One of Jackson's aides cried out in smoky twilight, "Cease firing! You are firing into your own men!" But an officer among the confused Confederates cried, "Who gave that order? It's a lie! Pour it into them, boys!" [61] And pour it in, they did, killing two men instantly and nearly ripping off Jackson's left arm at the shoulder.

The arm had to be amputated that night, causing General Lee to mourn, "General Jackson has lost his left arm but I have lost my right." Despite indications that he might yet recover, Jackson instead contracted pneumonia and was unmistakably drifting toward death on the eighth day following his wounding. When told that he probably would not survive until dusk, he responded characteristically, "Very good, it is all right. I always wanted to die on a Sunday. It will be an infinite gain to be translated to heaven." A little later, he closed his eyes and murmured his last words, "Let us cross over the river and rest under the shade of the trees." [62] Then he died at the age of thirty-nine.

A Legend and a Legacy

The South reacted passionately to the loss of their morale-boosting general. Newspapers compared him to Alexander the Great, Hannibal, Julius Caesar, Napoleon, Frederick of Prussia, and George Washington. They called him a Maker of Destiny, a Master of War, a paragon of Southern virtue. One tearful young woman mused, "He cannot die—he is an immortal reality." [63]

Upon announcing the news of Jackson's death to his men, one of the general's staff officers reflected, "The sounds of merriment in camp died away as if the Angel of Death himself had flapped his muffled wings over the troops." [64] And indeed it had. Even among

Confederate artillerymen lie dead in a field at the site of Antietam. Even though the battle resulted in the deaths of thousands, Jackson thanked God for the hard-earned draw.

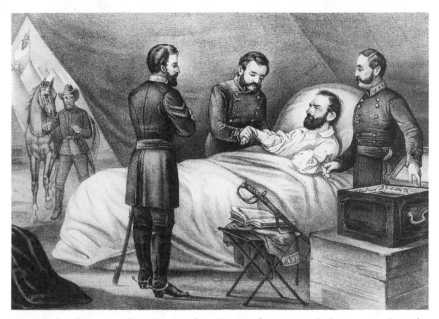

Medical aides attend to General Jackson after wounds he incurred at the battle at Chancellorsville forced doctors to amputate his left arm. Jackson died eight days after the battle and was greatly missed by Lee and the whole of the Confederate army.

the Northern soldiers where the name Stonewall Jackson had long inspired a terrible dread, men spoke respectfully of their departed opponent, though they did so with a decided tone of relief.

Thomas Jackson's influence continued through many years and, in fact, continues to be felt today. During World War II, commanders such as the American general George S. Patton and German field marshal Erwin Rommel conducted operations inspired by Jackson's rapid troop deployment, feints, and flanking maneuvers. General "Stormin'" Norman Schwarzkopf based the lightning-swift flanking tactics of the Persian Gulf War (Operation Desert Storm) in large part on Stonewall's campaigns. And military officers and cadets from all over the world still travel to the Shenandoah Valley in Virginia to learn from Jackson's triumphs there.

But perhaps the most lasting legacy that Thomas Jonathan Jackson left is the confirmation that seemingly ordinary people, indeed, people thoroughly tangled by eccentricities, can rise to greatness and even be propelled to it by those same quirks and the very "foolishness" they generate. For "Old Tom Fool," one of the clumsiest, most graceless hillbillies ever to stumble down the mountains of West Virginia, will stand forever among the great military leaders.

CHAPTER 4

James Longstreet:
Heroic Villain

Gainesville, Georgia
Autumn 1897

Former Confederate general James Longstreet threw down the newspaper and slammed his huge fist on the kitchen table. Nearly seventy-seven years old, he remained a bear of a man at six feet, two inches tall and 240 pounds in spite of old war wounds that had permanently disabled his thigh, throat, and right arm. His red-veined complexion and fiery eyes offered proof that his warrior's temperament was still intact despite his handicaps, and his Santa Claus beard did little to make him look jolly.

The old general rasped to his wife that the newspapers were bedeviling him again, still blaming him for losing at Gettysburg and losing the entire war, and all for simply speaking frankly about General Lee.

His second wife, a young and slender belle, glided into the kitchen and began soothing her husband's right shoulder and arm. She told him what he already knew, that the journalistic wolves were sure to have come after him all over again when he published his memoirs.

Longstreet protested to her that all he did was relay what he had witnessed, the way it had happened. And, in his opinion, General Lee had shown poor judgment at Gettysburg by ordering Pickett's disastrous frontal assault. He simply could not understand why he was the one who kept getting blamed for it.

Helen Gortch Longstreet, the general's recent bride, massaged her husband's spine as she often did and tried to comfort him by encouraging him to ignore what the editors and other generals wrote. She told him that General Lee probably had very little to do with it and that his enemies were really attacking him for becoming a Republican and taking jobs in the Reconstruction government and for trying to help the ex-slaves to vote.

The general attempted to rotate the stiffness out of his bullish neck and added that they never had let him forget his association with U.S. general and then president Ulysses S. Grant. Since their West Point days together, they had been the closest of friends. They had stopped seeing each other during the war and had not renewed their friendship until after it. Longstreet could not see any shame in that.

But it all made the aging general tired now to think how matters could have ever come to this, how the Southern people could have made him such a hero during the war and such a villain afterward. Young Helen, who would devote her entire life to clearing her husband's name and reputation, assured him that she would someday write the definitive book on the subject of Longstreet's contributions to the South, which is exactly what she did. General Longstreet knew how lucky he was to have such a dutiful and dedicated wife and he told her so again and again, but low points like these (and there were many in the general's long life) made him sag his heavy head into his hands and wonder how his life of selfless service to both nations to which he had sworn allegiance could have led him to such despair.

One Tough Young Man

James Longstreet descended from some of the earliest American colonists in New Amsterdam (later New York) and Massachusetts. His ancestors had always tended toward independence and self-reliance. Roving freely, they wound up living in the hill country between northwest Georgia and southwest South Carolina. James was born on the South Carolina side of that border on January 8, 1821, but stayed there only a few weeks before his parents moved to Georgia.

Young James's father nicknamed him "Peter" or "Pete" due to the boy's rocklike physique and stony will. Jesus had called his disciple Peter "the rock upon which I will build my church" and James's father had read that verse in the Bible enough times to find it fitting. Little Pete spent his earliest childhood in wild, reckless, wilderness—hiking, hunting, fishing, and of course working on his father's modest cotton plantation. Before the age of eight, he had developed the ability to think freely, trust in his survival skills, and endure enormous physical exertion. He had also learned when to speak, when to remain silent, and how to express himself with a straightforward honesty that many perceived as bluntness.

All of these qualities were mightily tested when Pete's father, who valued a good education, sent his nine-year-old to a private boarding school, the Richmond County (Georgia) Academy, renowned for its demanding curriculum and harsh conditions. After several years of icy baths, tasteless food, and welt-raising whippings, young James Longstreet moved to Alabama with his recently widowed mother, his father having died of natural causes. There he earned an appointment to the United States Military Academy at West Point, New York. The year was 1838. Not surprisingly, he found West Point's notoriously difficult physical regimen relatively easy compared to the prep school he had attended in Georgia. The academics at West Point, however, proved to be considerably more challenging.

More Soldier than Scholar

At "the Point," Cadet Longstreet reveled in sports. Whenever the call came to play, he was always first on the field, jostling his fellow cadets for the ball and challenging all comers regardless of the game. He entered the school measuring six feet, two inches tall and weighing 220 pounds, a virtual Goliath by the standards of the day. And his rollicking sense of adventure made him an instant leader when it came time for athletics.

No one could have said the same regarding his academics. He later wrote, "I had more interest in the school of the soldier, horsemanship, sword exercise, and the outside game of foot-ball than in the academic courses." [65] Throughout all four years at the academy, Pete Longstreet grappled with the mysteries of chemistry,

Cadets go through their morning drill at West Point academy. While Longstreet excelled at the physical regimen demanded of the cadets, he had a difficult time with the academic regimen.

French, English grammar, mechanics, and philosophy with only marginal success. He performed slightly better in the military science coursework but only well enough to graduate fifty-fourth among the fifty-six cadets in the class of 1842.

Pete Longstreet's greatest legacy at West Point was his popularity with the other cadets, the way in which he could lead them in a good time. He himself admitted, "As I was of a large and robust physique, I was at the head of most larks and games."[66] Those pranks cost him a significant number of demerits, a number that almost resulted in his expulsion from the academy. He never committed a serious crime, though, such as theft, cheating, or telling an outright lie. Most of his offenses were simply efforts to relieve the excruciating boredom all the cadets suffered due to their repetitious schedule. Led by Longstreet, cadets would sneak off the post to a local bar, play poker, and orchestrate loud, laughing pranks during study times.

Perhaps, though, "Old Pete" committed his worst offense when he befriended a shy underclassman from Ohio whom he described as being "of noble, generous heart, a lovable character, a valued friend."[67] That frail boy was Ulysses S. Grant, and their enduring camaraderie would eventually cause Longstreet years of aggravation. But that would not come for decades. In the meantime, there was a country to be served.

Soldiering in Federal Blue

Lieutenant James Longstreet spent the years from 1842 to 1846 bouncing from one desolate fort to the next, filling the boring hours with official duties such as drills, inspections, and an occasional field maneuver. At Jefferson Barracks in St. Louis, he was at least able to enjoy poker in his free time with his old friend Ulysses S. "Sam" Grant, who had also been stationed there. He, in fact, introduced the intensely shy Grant to his cousin, Julia Dent, and the two were eventually married. But first, Pete Longstreet mustered the courage to court and marry his commanding officer's daughter, Louisa Garland.

From St. Louis, Lieutenant Longstreet's duties as a professional soldier took him to Louisiana, Florida, and then Corpus Christi, Texas, where he once again met up with Sam Grant. The two comrades hunted and played a type of poker called "brag" every chance they got. The liquor often flowed freely and, whether they took advantage of them or not, the Mexican border town offered some of the most raucous gambling and prostitution houses in all the West.

Longstreet's combat experience during the Mexican-American War would be used to advantage during the Civil War. His bravery and calm leadership, as well as his avoidance of standard frontal assaults would prove invaluable during future conflicts.

Tactical Lessons Learned

The fun ended in 1846 when the United States went to war with Mexico to extend its borders into what is now southern Texas, Arizona, New Mexico, Utah, Nevada, Colorado, and California. In the bloody Mexican War that ensued, Longstreet threw himself into several desperate battles and grabbed two promotions due to his exemplary bravery and coolness under fire. He also learned tactical lessons that would carry him all the way through the Civil War.

Most important, he discovered firsthand that frontal assaults cost the attackers far too many lives and that flanking movements could gain the same results with fewer casualties. Even more significantly, he saw that battles could be won with the very fewest casualties by enticing the enemy to attack deeply entrenched defensive positions when the flanks, or sides, were anchored to easily defended terrain.

Ironically, however, Longstreet earned his greatest glory (and greatest suffering) in a frontal assault. His generals unleashed it against the Mexican fortress at Chapultepec just outside Mexico City. He had already earned the rank of captain for leading one successful charge, waving the flag to inspire his men. At Chapultepec, he found his troops similarly stalled before a fusillade of Mexican musketry and he did not hesitate to again rally them up the hill.

He grabbed the American flag and waved it furiously, hoping to steel the frayed nerves of his men. Then he sprinted off toward the fortress determined to seize it alone if no one else would follow him. Witnessing such bravado, his cheering troops fell in behind him and swarmed up the slope. Longstreet had led them almost to the top when a musket ball ripped through his thigh, sending him crashing to the ground. With jaw-clenching pain, he urged his men

U.S. troops storm the fortress of Chapultepec just outside Mexico City on September 13, 1846. Longstreet led a frontal assault on the fortress, helping to encourage his troops to victory.

on and managed to pass the flag to another officer who led the rush the rest of the way and swept the Mexicans from their fortress.

Descent into "Real" War

Longstreet made major for his gallantry at Chapultepec and began a well-earned convalescence. The United States went on to win the two-year war, stripping Mexico of one-third of its territory while suffering "acceptable" casualties. The major and his four children spent the next twelve years of relative peace at lonely outposts across the newly won territories as well as more established forts in the East and South. He eventually found himself riding a desk as an army paymaster in the New Mexico territory, more concerned about paying for his children's education than doing battle.

For years, though, Major Longstreet had been monitoring the expanding rift between the North and the South over states' rights, slavery, and a sticky web of related issues. Virtual warfare had already been raging throughout the 1850s in "Bleeding Kansas." When the Civil War finally boiled over into a full-scale battle at Fort Sumter in Charleston, South Carolina's harbor, he already knew what he, as a Georgian, would do. He resigned his commission as a major in the U.S. Army, accepted one as a lieutenant colonel in the Confederate army, and immediately set out for the Confederate capital at Richmond, Virginia, in search of a combat command.

Traits Surface for Better and Worse

Southern president Jefferson Davis and his military adviser, General Robert E. Lee, correctly surmised that the first Union invasion would come along the northern Virginia border near Washington, D.C. They sent twenty thousand men under General Pierre G. T. Beauregard to Manassas Junction to establish a defensive line along the south bank of a sluggish little creek called Bull Run. Another fifteen thousand men dug in at nearby Harpers Ferry. Recently promoted Brigadier General James Longstreet took command of the brigade (approximately twenty-five hundred Virginians) guarding the knee-deep crossing at Blackburn's Ford of Bull Run. As luck, good or bad, would have it, the Yankees launched their first attack precisely at that point on July 18, 1861, three days before the all-out engagement that would be called the First Battle of Manassas (or Bull Run).

The Battle of Blackburn's Ford would later be considered a mere skirmish compared to Shiloh, Antietam, and Gettysburg. Combined, the two sides at Blackburn's could only muster about

7,000 soldiers (150,000 fought at Gettysburg), but to the officers and men who had never before endured combat, which included the vast majority, this first engagement seemed an unwakable nightmare.

Keeping the Calm

After spending several days supervising the digging of formidable earthworks, General Longstreet's greatest challenge became keeping his raw recruits behind them. Many of his soldiers cracked and ran as soon as the shooting began. As Longstreet understated it, "The first pouring-down volleys were most startling to the new troops." [68] But all day long he calmly rode and walked among them, exposing himself to the fusillades, cigar in mouth, saber in hand, and emboldening words pouring from his heart.

And when the sun finally retreated behind the hills, so did the last attacking wave of Union soldiers. Longstreet had held his line and important Confederates heard about it. One brigade commander who witnessed the fight reported back to Richmond, "Longstreet was actively engaged in the thickest of the fire in directing and encouraging the men under his command, and I am satisfied that he contributed largely to the repulse of the enemy by his own personal exertions." [69] Although he did not participate during the larger Rebel victory three days later, Longstreet had made his mark as a scrappy general and he would be called upon again.

Little battling of consequence took place along the Manassas line from August 1861 through May 1862, though the surly Longstreet drilled, marched, and otherwise disciplined his men relentlessly. After hours, however, his headquarters became the center of officer conviviality, a place where laughter, good food, poker, and whiskey could be counted on to counteract the monotony of the bivouac, or war camp. One of Longstreet's aides described him during this time as being

> one of the kindest, best hearted men I ever knew. Those not acquainted with him think him short and crabbed and he does appear so except in three places: 1st, when in the presence of ladies, 2nd, at the table, and 3rd, on the field of battle. At any of those places he has a complacent smile on his countenance, and seems to be one of the happiest men in the world. [70]

But that happiness turned to a brooding grief and bitterness from which he never completely recovered when three of his cherished children died of scarlet fever. Never having been one to share his pain with others, he tried to swallow his anguish but it ended up swallowing him. He returned to duty far earlier than anyone thought wise but work was apparently all that could console him. It was months before he again hosted his fellow generals at his headquarters and, even then, he withdrew and took no part in the high jinks.

Advances and Retreats

Longstreet's depression may have worsened his lackluster performance early in the Peninsular campaign of March to July 1862. According to an aide, "in a fight he was a man of but very few words, and kept at all times his own counsels."[71] After the deaths of his children he became dangerously withdrawn and uncommunicative in battle.

At the Battle of Seven Pines just east of Richmond, this silence contributed to several costly errors. He advanced his division (he was by then a major general) along roads earmarked for other commands and marched his fourteen thousand men across a single-file bridge rather than constructing a wider one to speed the crossing. He gave unclear orders to subordinates and failed to capitalize on enemy weaknesses described by his cavalry scouts. In so doing, he helped cause critical delays and ill-placed thrusts that contributed to the atrociously large number of Confederates killed and wounded and turned a probable victory into a draw at best.

Certainly other generals (notably Stonewall Jackson) made blunders on the peninsula over the next few weeks as the Confederates, now under Robert E. Lee, bludgeoned the Unionists from southeastern Virginia. But Longstreet seemed quicker to blame others for his own failures and he sometimes took credit for successful ideas that he had not suggested. In spite of gaining the confidence of General Lee during the clumsy bloodbath known as the Seven Days' Battle, he knew that he would have to do something worthy of commendation to fully restore his name and reputation. And he got his chance at summer's end on the same battlefield where he had achieved his initial glory a year earlier.

Promotion and Commotion

General Robert E. Lee regarded the "win" at the Seven Days' Battle as an ugly victory that revealed only a few Rebel generals with enough talent to serve as his top lieutenants. After reorganizing his forces into just two large commands, he chose Thomas "Stonewall" Jackson to lead one and James Longstreet to lead the other. Lee said of "Old Pete" that "he was the staff in my right hand."[72] Longstreet himself described their developing relationship as being one of "confidence and esteem, official and personal, which was ripening into stronger ties as the mutations of war bore heavier upon us."[73]

That may have been true while they actively campaigned but, in camp during times of relative peace, Pete Longstreet was often a grumpy bear whose tender ego caused nearly as many headaches for the fatherly Lee as the Yankees themselves. While still bivouacked near Richmond, Longstreet read an article in a newspaper that gave General A. P. Hill credit for a victory that he thought he should have received. Both generals behaved badly until a feud erupted between them that resulted in Longstreet arresting Hill, the fiery Hill calling for a duel, and General Lee transferring Hill to Jackson's command.

General A. P. Hill (pictured) made an enemy of Longstreet after he received credit for a victory Longstreet felt was his own. Their disagreement resulted in Lee reappointing Hill to Stonewall Jackson's command.

Shortly thereafter, Longstreet arrested another of his generals, a former politician named Robert Toombs. General Toombs had not posted pickets (guards) around his camp. This definitely warranted some type of disciplinary action, but Longstreet refused Lee's moderate suggestions for punishment and would not relent until he had thoroughly disgraced Toombs.

Victory and More Controversy

Pete Longstreet craved a battle into which he could release his anger, and he got it. A new Union army under John Pope was slowly making its way south from Washington and was already in the middle of Virginia. Over the next four weeks, Longstreet moved his newly formed command (more than half of Lee's Army of Northern Virginia) north to meet the threat. Meanwhile Jackson maneuvered the rest of the Confederate army around Pope's right flank to strike the Yankees' rear.

In late August, Stonewall surprise-attacked Pope's supply depot and then ran for defensive cover behind an unfinished railroad grade on the old Manassas battleground. Pope fell back fuming for Jackson and, when he found him, launched an evening and a day's worth of frontal assaults. Jackson's outnumbered men just barely held on waiting for Longstreet to come up and plow into the fray alongside him but Old Pete did not come as expected on the first morning. Nor did he make it by midday. And even when he did arrive in the late afternoon he did not attack, choosing instead to study the ground and appraise the situation. Longstreet later wrote, "The position was not inviting and I so reported to General Lee. I suggested, as the day was far spent, that a reconnaissance be made at nightfall."[74] Frustrated by Old Pete's overcaution and worried about Jackson's men, Lee hesitantly postponed the attack.

Union commander John Pope (pictured) faced Jackson and Longstreet outside Virginia. Although Longstreet's reinforcement of Jackson's troops resulted in a Confederate victory, many accused Longstreet of being overly cautious in the battle.

Longstreet listened from a few miles away as Jackson's command fought on like a buzz saw, tearing into the Yankees with rocks, clubs, and fingernails when their ammunition ran out. When General Longstreet finally did unleash his attack the next afternoon, riding before his men "like a king leading his hosts to battle,"[75] he beat the Unionists and drove the survivors back to Washington. It was a great victory for Longstreet but once again it was marred by charges that he had hesitated before going in, that he had been too careful. He shrugged off the complaints, though, and mollified Lee who was admittedly "greatly disappointed"[76] that his delays had cost Jackson's men such an extended agony. But Lee was just as greatly pleased with the panic that Longstreet had eventually inflicted on the Union ranks.

A Genius for Defense

The Maryland campaign came next during which Lee boldly divided his already undersized army into four smaller sections to carry out diverse and isolated missions. In keeping with his cautious nature, General Longstreet protested to Lee about the plan. He later wrote, "I objected that the move would be very imprudent as we were then in the enemy's country, that he would be advised within ten or twelve hours of our movements, and would surely move out against us in our dispersed condition."[77]

Longstreet's concerns took on even greater urgency when a copy of Lee's orders fell into the hands of the Union commander, George McClellan. Only luck, McClellan's ineptitude, and desperate fighting on the part of the Confederates kept the worst of Longstreet's fears from materializing at Sharpsburg, Maryland, near Antietam Creek.

Throughout that cataclysm on September 17, 1862, General Longstreet and his half of the Army of Northern Virginia defended the middle and right of Lee's line against dozens of lacerating attacks. At a sunken farm road renamed Bloody Lane shortly thereafter, he personally directed the desperate stand and even helped to man an artillery piece when all of its crew had been killed. In the heat of this hands-on battling, one witness said Old Pete rode or strode about "with perfect indifference to the bursting shells."[78] Others remarked, "he was as cool and composed as if on dress parade"[79] and "I could discover no trace of unusual excitement except that he seemed to cut through his cigar at each chew."[80]

Perhaps one of his aides summed up Longstreet's warrior presence best when he wrote,

He seemed everywhere along his extended lines, and his tenacity and deep-set resolution, his inmost courage which appeared to swell with the growing peril to the army undoubtedly stimulated the troops to greater action, and held them in place despite all weakness.[81]

For whatever reason, Longstreet held his ground in spite of losing 40 percent of his men. Jackson barely clung to his position on the left as well and together they bought just enough time for reinforcements to arrive late in the day and end the battle in a draw.

A New Name and a New Role

Old Pete's iron-willed tenacity at Bloody Lane did not go unnoticed by General Lee and it earned him yet another nickname. "My Old War Horse," Longstreet began to hear the commanding general call him, due in large measure to his tight-gutted defense. The next spate of battles capitalized on that strength, perhaps most notably behind the infamous stone wall at Fredericksburg, Virginia. Anticipating Union general Ambrose Burnside's foolhardy attempts to frontally advance his thousands up steep, open ground, Longstreet coolly reported to Lee that "if they put every man on that field and approach me over the same line, and you give me plenty of ammunition, I will kill them all before they reach my line."[82] Which is nearly what happened during the frigid snow squalls of December 13, 1862. The attacking Unionists lost twelve thousand brave, obedient men. The defending Rebels lost half that number.

Soon after the Battle of Fredericksburg, General Lee sent Longstreet on an independent assignment in southeast Virginia to protect Richmond from threatening Yankee troops, but the mission went awry from the start. Old Pete could not lure the Unionists into attacking his forbidding defensive positions like they had at Fredericksburg. While awaiting an assault that never came, he missed Lee and Jackson's fabled offensive at Chancellorsville in May 1863 but rejoined Lee in time for his second invasion of the North.

After Stonewall Jackson's death at Chancellorsville, Longstreet became even more important to General Lee both personally and professionally. Now Old Pete the War Horse was Lee's closest confidant and adviser and his most reliable field commander. But in early July 1863, at a little town called Gettysburg, stresses appeared in their relationship that would eventually ruin Longstreet's reputation. His passion for defense, his natural caution, and his long-standing habit of speaking his mind bluntly were about to make him numerous enemies.

The Battle That Never Ended

The first three days of July 1863 proved to be the most horrible days of the Civil War. Fifty thousand bright-eyed, vital young men and boys either died, suffered terrible wounds, or languished in the hunger, sickness, and degradation of captivity for the remainder of the war. South-central Pennsylvania might have hosted this battle, but surely it had its origins in the underworld.

The first day saw the Confederates drive the Unionists from the fields and village up onto the high ground running south of town, which included Culp's Hill, Cemetery Ridge, Little Round Top, and Big Round Top. Nightfall stopped plans for the Southerners to cast the Yankees from those hills before they could dig in, but subsequent Union reinforcements arrived before morning and they were able to harden their positions.

An observer from the British army had remarked that "Longstreet is never far from General Lee, who relies very much upon his judgment."[83] Longstreet's judgment in this case included his desire to outflank the high ground altogether and get behind the Union army somewhere between it and Washington, D.C., less than one hundred miles away. Such a threat to the Union capital, he reasoned, would force the Yankees down into the open and require them to frontally attack the heavily defended high ground of the Confederates' choosing.

As sound as the plan appeared, General Lee pointed to the fortified hills and flushed red with rare anger. "General Longstreet, if the enemy is there tomorrow, we must attack him!" Longstreet fired back, "If he is there, it will be because he is anxious that we should attack him—a good reason, in my judgment, for not doing so."[84]

Surprising no one, the Northerners were still there as the second day of battle commenced and Longstreet received his orders from General Lee to launch a morning assault against them from the Confederate right. The War Horse did not, however, get his men off until later in the afternoon, taking too long to plan and execute his troop movements. Once in motion, he had to march and countermarch his men when their road veered too close to Union signal-flagmen on a tower, who would have spotted them and called in artillery fire. And as always, naked frontal assaults simply cut against his grain. As he put it later, "I realized that our losses would be so heavy when we attacked that our army must soon be depleted to such an extent that we should not be able to hold a force in the field sufficient to meet our adversary." [85] All these reasons notwithstanding, it is undeniable that his delay threw off the timing of the other attacks involved in General Lee's plan and diminished whatever chances any of them might have had for success.

Consequently, the Union lines held on the second day despite some of the most brutal fighting ever displayed by humankind. On the third day, General Lee ordered a fifteen-thousand-man division under George Pickett (part of General Longstreet's command) to charge straight across a mile-long, open field directly into the artillery and blazing rifles of twenty thousand Yankees. Old Pete wrote,

> I felt then that it was my duty to express my convictions; I said "General, I have been a soldier all my life. I have been with soldiers engaged in fights by couples, by squads, companies, regiments, divisions, and armies, and should know, as well as any one, what soldiers can do. It is my opinion that no fifteen thousand men ever arranged for battle can take that position." [86]

Lee emphatically disagreed and commanded Longstreet to launch Pickett's Charge, which ultimately destroyed the Confederate States of America's hopes of independence.

Delaying the Inevitable

Many more battles were fought over the remaining two years of the war, including one at Chickamauga in northwest Georgia just two months after Gettysburg, which proved to be General Longstreet's greatest command victory and a wholesale defeat for the Union. However, two months after that, Old Pete led another independent command in a winter campaign to drive the Yankees from the mountains around Knoxville in eastern Tennessee. That effort turned out to be not only Longstreet's worst showing personally but the Confederates' poorest performance of the entire war. Afterward, a depressed Longstreet tendered his resignation to Jefferson Davis, a gesture which the Confederate president promptly rejected.

At the Battle of the Wilderness in Virginia (May 1864), he was in the process of regaining some of his reputation. Then, in the swirling smoke and chaos of combat, some of his own men accidentally shot him through the neck and right shoulder. He recov-

Longstreet gives General Pickett the order to charge at Gettysburg. Pickett's Charge resulted in a massive loss of life that severely damaged the strength of Confederate troops and ruined their hopes of winning the war.

ered (minus his once-booming voice and the use of his right arm) in time to rejoin Robert E. Lee for the last-ditch defense of Petersburg and Richmond from June 1864 through April 1865. He eventually surrendered with Lee on April 9 at Appomattox Court House, Virginia.

Then the second war started, featuring the publication of former Confederate generals' books, articles, speeches, and letters to editors. The objective of this second war was to determine who among them could most readily be cinched and saddled with the

Troops engage in battle at Chicamauga, Georgia, where Longstreet would win his greatest victory.

burden of losing the war. And it was James Longstreet who, by his actions after the war, had the chafing bit of blame pulled hardest into his mouth.

From Gold to Rusted Scrap

James Longstreet had always been a pragmatic man, one driven more by practicalities and common sense than by ideals and abstract virtues. As the war ended and large parts of the South smoldered in ruins, he knew that he had a wife and seven children to support so he moved to one of the only Southern cities that was still thriving: New Orleans. One of the reasons for the Crescent City's economic boom was that it had been captured without being destroyed early in the war and the Union occupation forces had fostered growth and opportunity for "reconstructed" Southern men.

Longstreet soon determined just what "reconstructed" would mean to him. He would have to cooperate with and eventually work for the very people who had recently invaded and destroyed his homeland. Untroubled by the pride and indignation that infused so many former Rebel officers, he quickly became a member of the late Mr. Lincoln's hated Republican Party and undertook a long progression of political patronage jobs reserved for what loyal Southerners called collaborators and abolitionists.

The jobs included surveyor of the port of New Orleans, U.S. marshal, federal postmaster, and even minister (ambassador) to Turkey. Once he strained his relations with his fellow Southerners to the point of breaking. As adjutant general of the primarily black state militia, he led an attack that killed several former Rebel soldiers attempting to take over government buildings in New Orleans.

To make matters worse as far as the "unreconstructed" Rebels were concerned, Longstreet publically renewed his old friendship with the so-called "villainous" general and then U.S. president Ulysses S. Grant. Longstreet called him "the truest as well as the bravest man who ever lived; my lifetime personal friend who has always been kindest when I have been most fiercely assaulted." [87] He defended the reviled Grant in speech and print and openly supported his "Black Republican" policies, even going so far as to

Longstreet's cooperation with Reconstruction led him to be maligned and hated in his native South.

canvass for the ex-slaves' right to vote. That was simply too much for ardent ex-Confederates to bear. They labeled Longstreet a scalawag, a Southerner bent on taking advantage of the down-trodden whites. Other scornful epithets such as traitor, Judas, and leper shot at him like so many cannonballs but he endured the barrage to provide his still-growing family with food, shelter, and clothing.

The War Goes On

Former Confederate generals, many of whom had been his close comrades during the war, quickly began to attack his performance as a battlefield commander. They unearthed his mistakes and smeared them about in books, articles, and speeches. Within a few years, his enemies had blown his wartime misjudgments into the sole cause for the Confederate defeat. Longstreet made the situation worse by responding in bitter letters to newspaper editors and eventually in his memoirs.

In the process, he committed the most egregious, that is, shame-ful, Southern crime. He criticized the demigod Robert E. Lee, even suggesting that "Lee's headlong combativeness would not let the battle end until blood enough was shed to appease him." [88] He also asserted that Lee's insistence at Gettysburg to attack frontally, not his own sluggishness, had cost the Confederacy the battle and the war.

Although history has borne out many of Longstreet's allega-tions, they were at the time tantamount to treason if not complete sacrilege to all loyal Southerners, and few among them ever for-gave him. Instead, Old Pete, Lee's War Horse, had to spend the rest of his long life assailed by detractors who blamed him for the Confederate army's failure. He lived out his last years on a farm with his young and beautiful second wife, Helen, growing grapes and making wine. He was clearly sad and embittered about the way his life had turned out. Nearing the end, he beckoned death to relieve him. "My arm," he complained, "is paralyzed, my voice that once could be heard all along the lines is gone, my hearing is very much impaired, and I sometimes wish the end would come." [89]

Peace at Last

And the end did come in 1904 when he was eighty-six, but not be-fore he was finally invited to a Rebel function, in this case the un-veiling of a war memorial. A throng of ex-Confederates attended, many of whom had fought under him in their youth. Understand-ably anxious about how they would receive him, the creaking

Longstreet slowly began the long walk to the middle of the stage. The crowd was silent at first, but then he heard a single pair of hands start to clap. More and more hands swelled the ovation until cheering erupted as well. By the time he had tottered to center stage, these men were shrilling the Rebel yell as best they could remember and perform it. Longstreet, still uncertain, leaned over to another former general and asked what the commotion was all about. The other general grasped Longstreet's hand and said, "Why, Pete, don't you know? They are cheering for you." Overwhelmed, Lee's one-time War Horse lowered his eyes and wept.

CHAPTER 5

James Ewell Brown Stuart: The Happy Cavalier

The Virginia Peninsula Near Richmond

On the night of June 10, 1862, General James Ewell Brown (Jeb) Stuart left Robert E. Lee's headquarters tent, camped on the Virginia peninsula near Richmond. Stuart clutched a set of orders and grinned across the full width of his bushy, red beard. He had finally talked Lee into approving his plan to take twelve hundred of his toughest cavalrymen on a wild reconnaissance raid completely around General George McClellan's approaching Union army. Stuart was bursting to tell someone about it. But he knew the importance of secrecy in the undertaking so he stifled his joy and settled for reading Lee's orders again:

> You are desired to make a scout movement to the rear of the enemy, now posted on the Chickahominy River, with a view of gaining intelligence of his size, operations, communications, etc., and of driving in his foraging parties and securing such grain, cattle, etc., for ourselves as you can make arrangements to have driven in. Another object is to destroy his wagon trains.

Since former West Point commandant Lee remembered Cadet Stuart's fearlessness from a decade earlier, Lee also added, "You will return as soon as the object of your expedition is accomplished, and you must bear in mind, while endeavoring to execute the general purpose of your mission, not to hazard unnecessarily your command." [90]

Within a couple of hours, Stuart was riding at the head of his entourage, singing loudly and spurring his sweaty mount into a gallop at every chance. This was war to twenty-eight-year-old Jeb

Stuart: the hunt, the chase, flying headlong into danger, the fear of death never darkening his soul. A staff officer thundering to keep up with him later wrote,

> As he rode his horse he was a gallant figure to look at. The gray coat buttoned to the chin, the light French saber, the pistol in its black holster; cavalry boots above the knee, and the brown hat with its black plume soaring above the bearded features, the brilliant blue eyes and the huge mustache, which curled with laughter at the slightest provocation—they made Stuart the perfect picture of a cavalier, and the spirited horse he rode seemed to feel that he carried one whose motto was to "do or die." [91]

General J. E. B. Stuart leads his cavalry in his famous ride around McClellan's troops. Stuart's almost careless bravery won him the respect and admiration of Lee, who called him the eyes and ears of his army.

Stuart and his men first encountered Union cavalry about noon in the fields around Totopottomy Creek. In the pursuit that broke out, the Rebels "dashed on, here skirting a field, there leaping a fence or ditch and clearing the woods beyond, when, not far from Old Church, the enemy made a stand, having been reinforced." [92] The ensuing collision of some three thousand horsemen clanged with saber steel and popped with pistol shots; the rotten-egg smell of gunpowder singed their nostrils. Frightened horses screamed and spit froth while a muddy stench was kicked up from thousands of agitated hooves.

After a few eternal minutes, the Unionists panicked and fled for their lives. General Stuart ordered another yip-yipping chase but called it off when they overtook the enemies' abandoned camp. Booty, he had often said, was good for a cavalryman's morale. Stuart watched approvingly as his young Rebels laughed and cheered, gorging themselves with beef, hams, and canned lobsters from Maine, but he eventually had to remind them that they were not yet halfway through their odyssey and now the Yankees were alerted to their presence. There would be many tight scrapes ahead, he shouted to them, crossings of flooded rivers, attacks by growing numbers of cavalry and running the gauntlet of gunboats and field artillery. Though he did not say it, he knew that the greatest hardship would be the fatigue of riding and fighting for three excruciating days without the luxury of sleep.

"Asleep in the Saddle"

As the night-and-day, day-and-night running skirmish progressed, one of his aides noticed that often "whole companies were asleep in the saddle, and Stuart was no exception. At one point, he had thrown one knee over the pommel of his saddle, folded his arms, dropped his bridle, and—chin on breast, his plumed hat drooping over his forehead—was sound asleep." [93]

Near the end of the third day, only one more swollen river stood between the raiders and the safety of their own lines. Despite their aching exhaustion, they managed to cross it. And then they were home, they were heroes, and the information for which they had risked so much instantly enhanced Lee's chances of throwing the Unionists back into the sea. Even more than that, the audacity and flamboyance of Stuart's "ride around McClellan" bolstered the limp morale of the entire Southern Confederacy. By boldly thumbing his nose at 115,000 embarrassed Federals with his mere 1,200 Confederates, Stuart gave credence to the long-standing boast that "one Southern boy was worth ten Yankees" or, in this case, a hundred.

It would take many stalemates and defeats later in the war to change the Southerners' view of their soldiers just after Stuart's raid. But they would never give up their love of the man who had allowed them that joy and pride in the beginning. And his life, even from childhood, would serve as their model of the ideal Confederate fighting man.

A Soldier from the Beginning

James Ewell Brown Stuart was born at his father's southwest Virginia plantation on February 6, 1833, and by midchildhood he was already a grizzled fighter. He once shinnied out a tree limb to battle a nest of swarming hornets and, gritting against the stings, he doggedly destroyed his objective and drove his enemy from the plantation. At about the same time, his reputation as a fistfighter was making it hard for him to find challenging takers from among the other planters' sons his own age so he had to take on older and bigger boys.

His combative spirit pleased his father but worried his devoutly Christian mother. She took the boy aside at age twelve and made him swear two oaths to her, both of which he never violated. He was to always love the Lord and, just as important, to abstain from drinking alcohol. The former he honored but not to the point of letting it crimp his fun; the latter he obeyed so thoroughly that he attempted to shun a dose of medicinal whiskey meant to ease the pain of the gunshot that slowly killed him.

Young Stuart displayed competence, if not brilliance, during his early education, remarking that his teachers "instilled their knowledge into me partly by the mouth and partly by the rod." [94] Despite his tendency toward misbehavior, he gained admission to West Point in 1850, where that misbehavior continued and nearly earned him enough demerits for expulsion. His principal offense was fighting. Although concerned, his father could not bring himself to completely discourage Jeb's combative nature. In one letter, he counseled,

> I much regret that you have been involved in another fighting scrape. My dear son, I can excuse more readily a fault more of the sort that you have committed, in which you maintained your character as a man of honor and courage, than almost any other. But I hope you will, hereafter, avoid getting into difficulties in which such maintainance must be demanded at your hands. [95]

No doubt, the elder Stuart's ambivalence was not lost on the younger Stuart.

Jeb managed to stay out of trouble long enough to graduate thirteenth in a class of forty-six and to be admired by at least one classmate for his "strict attention to his military duties, an erect, soldierly bearing, an immediate and almost thankful acceptance of a challenge from a cadet to fight, and a clear, metallic ringing voice." [96] He also left the Academy with a nickname that had hounded him through all four years there. "Beauty," his friends called him. Without the magnificent beard that would later enhance his large-featured face, the irony of the playful tease humored everybody except Jeb.

Although he was almost kicked out of West Point for fighting, Stuart behaved long enough to graduate and later became one of the most important generals for the Confederacy.

Indians, a Wife, and John Brown's Body

Upon graduation from West Point in 1854, Lieutenant Jeb Stuart lost no time in finding the fights he had always craved. He served with the mounted rifles and then the elite 1st U.S. Cavalry in their battles with Comanche and Apache Indians across Texas and the Kansas Territory. He nearly died once in an effort to save a comrade, taking a point-blank bullet in the chest meant for his friend. But the bullet did not unhorse Stuart, who killed the Indian rifleman with his razored saber. Two weeks later, he was back in the saddle searching for more Indians.

In Kansas, he fell recklessly in love with Flora Cooke, his commanding officer's daughter, and won her engagement after just three weeks of horseback rides together. They married there and, while the playful cavalier never lost his flair for flirting with a pretty lady, he remained faithful to Flora. The birth of their first child, a girl he named Flora after his beloved wife, further cemented their bond and satisfied a desire for which he had yearned even more than soldiering: a loving, close-knit family that would thereafter serve as his most solid support. A baby boy followed whom he named Philip after Flora's father.

Stuart also encountered another person in Kansas who would figure largely in his life. That person was "Ossawatomie" John Brown, the fanatical abolitionist, whom he helped to drive from the territory for murdering five people, some from the same family, all proslavery. Stuart returned to Washington in October 1859 to patent and sell an invention to the government that enabled cavalrymen to more quickly attach and detach their swords from their belts. While there, that same John Brown seized the federal arsenal at Harpers Ferry, Virginia (now West Virginia), in an attempt to start a slave insurrection.

Lieutenant Stuart accompanied his old West Point commandant Colonel Robert E. Lee and a detachment of U.S. Marines on a mission to arrest Brown. Once there, Lee sent Stuart to read the surrender demand to Brown and his handful of followers who had been trapped inside a small, brick fire engine house. Rifle in hand, Brown scoffed at young Stuart and his demand, saying later that, "I might have killed that lieutenant just as easily as I could a mosquito." [97] But it was Brown who would die after being captured in the assault that J. E. B. Stuart led, convicted for treason in a Virginia court of law and hung by the neck in a ten-foot drop from the gallows.

John Brown ascends the scaffold to be hanged. On the way to the gallows, Brown commented on the scenery—seemingly unperturbed by his imminent death.

War Is All Glory

John Brown had been right about one thing. Just before being executed for treason, he handed a scribbled note to a guard that included, "The sins of this land [slavery] shall not be purged except by blood." [98] And for Stuart, the blood began to flow in the summer of 1861. The attack of Fort Sumter brought the long sectional crisis to a head and the secession of Virginia caused then Captain Stuart to resign from the U.S. Army. When his father-in-law remained in the Union army, Jeb changed the name of his little boy from Philip to James Ewell Brown Stuart Jr., or Jemmie. Of the father-in-law whom he had once loved, Stuart said, "He will regret his decision but once and that will be continuously." [99]

Stuart, now twenty-eight, accepted a commission as captain in the newly-forming Confederate army. His first assignment was as Colonel Thomas J. Jackson's chief of cavalry, all 350 of them, at Harpers Ferry. Captain Stuart found war a perfect delight there, consisting of lightning raids, scouting behind enemy lines, and brief manic clashes with Federal cavalry. When dangers did not exist, he would invent them as he did once by single-handedly approaching fifty Union soldiers in a meadow and calling out in his most authoritative voice, "You are surrounded! Throw down your arms or you are dead men!" Bewildered, the Yankees did as they were told and Stuart marched them back to camp as prisoners.

Promoted to lieutenant colonel, Stuart took advantage of the quiet periods to train his volunteers in the ways of cavalier warfare. He once inflated himself to near-mythic stature on his horse and sounded out like a trumpet,

> Attention. Now I want to talk to you, men. You are brave fellows and patriotic, too, but you are ignorant of this kind of war and I am teaching you. I want you to observe that a good man and a good horse can never be caught. Another thing: cavalry can trot away from anything, and a gallop is unbecoming to a soldier, unless he is going toward the enemy. Remember that. We gallop toward the enemy, and trot away, always. And be steady. Never break ranks.[100]

As part of the training, Lieutenant Colonel Stuart often exposed his men to rifle and artillery fire simply to get them accustomed to it. He also charged them through overwhelming numbers of Union troops to teach them how to escape tight situations. But rather than grouse about their commander's seeming disregard for their safety, the troopers' sentiments, to a man, could be summed up by the one who wrote, "He never could be still. He was rarely in camp, and he never showed fatigue. He led almost everything and we would follow him anywhere." [101]

The Big Show

Strategically, Jeb Stuart's most significant contribution to the early Confederate war effort came when his small but mighty band of troopers screened the transfer of the Rebels at Harpers Ferry to Manassas. There they reinforced the Southerners to a strength capable of withstanding the main Union assault. Stuart initiated so many raids and clashes with Union probes and patrols near Harpers Ferry that the Union commander there was convinced that he still faced the bulk of Johnston's army. The tireless ploy worked so well that those twenty thousand Yankees never made it to Manassas for the First Battle of Bull Run. Stuart's men, however, arrived in time to anchor the left flank of Thomas J. Jackson's "stone wall" and slash the retreating Yankees halfway back to Washington.

When recommending Stuart's promotion to general afterward, Confederate commander Johnston wrote to President Jefferson Davis,

Colonel Stuart is a rare man, wonderfully endowed by nature with the qualities necessary for an officer of light cavalry. Calm, firm, acute, active, and enterprising, I know of no one more competent than he to estimate the occurrences before him at their true value. If you add a real brigade of cavalry to this army, you cannot find a better brigadier-general to command it.[102]

And so Davis promoted him, but not before another six months of relative inactivity along the northern Virginia front. Once again, Stuart passed the time much as he had at Harpers Ferry, training his troops with raids, reconnaissances, and dashes behind enemy lines. He even staged a horse race through several squads of rifle-firing Union pickets, or guards.

But all was not action. Every night (and also when he rode on missions) Jeb led his troops in joyous sing-alongs, accompanied by his banjo player, Sweeney. Flora and their two children often visited his camp, rendering Stuart the happiest man in Virginia. The camp was named Qui Vive, roughly translated from French as "Who goes there!" because his outpost was closest to the enemy. Such frivolity and devotion to family would later enhance his fame. However, it would not be until his June 1862 ride around McClellan on the Virginia peninsula that his name would become part of the Southern psyche.

A Gunboat and a Yankee Coat

The marshy terrain on the peninsula made large-scale cavalry operations impractical during Robert E. Lee's Seven Days' Battle to save Richmond. After circling McClellan's army, General Jeb Stuart and his troopers spent most of their time supporting infantry flanks and gathering much-needed intelligence. He did manage to break away and wrangle a little more glory for himself and his men by taking on a feared Yankee gunboat that had been preventing the Southerners' use of an important river.

Both sides considered boats such as this one to be impervious to ground attack due to their sturdy construction and huge guns. They also carried a contingent of sharpshooters capable of making amphibious landings to clear out pockets of resistance along riverbanks. All in all, the gunboats garnered great respect and no one dared approach them on foot. Not surprisingly, Jeb Stuart proved the exception.

Flying in the face of all accepted military doctrine of the day, he led a party of just seventy-five men with carbines across an open field in plain view of the gunboat. As Stuart hoped, the Yankee

General Stuart leads his men around McClellan's army on the Virginia peninsula. Stuart's ability to elude detection while performing reconnaissance greatly improved Lee's battle strategy.

landing party swarmed ashore only to be driven back in an ambush he had set for them. Stuart then placed one of his light artillery pieces so close to the riverbank that the boat's long-distance siege guns could not aim low enough to hit it or his men. Beneath a ceiling of deafening but ineffective Union firepower, the little cannon peppered the gunboat so furiously that it had to retreat far down the river with Jeb Stuart's tiny force harassing it the entire way. Little strategic damage was done to the Yankees by the defeat but Southern newspapers turned it into yet another morale booster for the Confederacy, gilding the reputation of Jeb Stuart all the more.

In a similarly audacious raid a few weeks later, Stuart led a small party behind the lines of a new Union army making its way down through the heartland of Virginia, this one commanded by the arrogant general John Pope. That man's boasting and mistreatment of civilians had made him an outcast even in the North, and the Southerners wanted nothing more than to see him brought down.

Stuart got the chance while scouting ahead of General Lee's Army of Northern Virginia as it marched northward to do battle with Pope (after having driven McClellan's Yankees from the peninsula during the Seven Days' Battle). Choosing what Jeb called "the darkest night I ever saw," [103] he and a few of his best men used directions from a helpful slave and groped their way into Pope's headquarters encampment at Catlett's Station. Stuart was disappointed to find that the Northern general was away at the time but he managed to make off with several of his personal

91

baggage wagons, one of which included the man's finest dress uniform. The resplendent blue suit found its way into the display window of a Richmond tailor shop where crowds of Southern patriots reveled in its owner's humiliation.

General Jeb Stuart had once again bolstered Rebel spirits while accruing even more accolades for himself. But during that summer of 1862, his innermost satisfaction and delight came during his family's frequent visits to his camps. He and Flora took long, hand-holding walks and rides together and the children played gleefully among the doting cavalrymen. Local plantation owners hosted them at night where Flora's guitar added to the laughing, singing, and dancing.

The Liberation of Virginia

However, work was work and Stuart continued to scout, take prisoners for interrogation, protect infantry flanks, guard mountain passes, shield large troop movements, and clash viciously with Union cavalry patrols sent out to do the same thing for their army. Near the battlefield at Manassas, he and his troopers also enjoyed the uncommon treat of raiding a Union supply depot behind General Pope's lines. They satiated their ravaging hunger and replaced their tattered garments with the best that the U.S. Army could provide.

One Confederate officer who witnessed the spree reported, "It was amusing to see here a ragged fellow regaling himself with a box of pickled oysters or potted lobster; there another cutting into a cheese of enormous size while hundreds were opening packages of boots and shoes and other clothing."[104]

The fun ended at the Second Battle of Manassas when, despite the resultant Confederate victory, ten thousand young Southerners (and thirteen thousand Northerners) either died or nearly died in two days of battle. Stuart still managed to excite the newspaper readers again, though, by craftily delaying an enemy advance with a ruse. He had his men drag tree branches behind them over the roads approaching an undefended Southern flank. The branches stirred up so much dust that the Yankee commanders mistook the cloud for an arriving Rebel army, and denied themselves an easy victory. In the time bought, General James Longstreet's corps did show up, plug the gap, and drive the Unionists from Virginia.

From Gowns to Gore in Maryland

Stuart (guarding Lee's right flank) capitalized on the Confederate momentum by leading his men across the Potomac River and into

Maryland in hopes of liberating the Southern sympathizing elements of that border state from what Robert E. Lee called the "yoke of Northern tyranny." While he found that the majority of Marylanders did not want such liberation, Jeb wooed at least some of them to the Rebel cause by hosting an impromptu Southern-style ball right under the noses of the pursuing Unionists.

With brass bands, floral wreathes, and flag bunting, he transformed an unused girls' academy into a tidewater mansion. Stuart then hosted the young ladies from the area (properly chaperoned, of course) to an all-night party of dancing and chivalrous gaiety. The repulse of a Union cavalry party that strayed nearby only added to the women's romantic zeal, prompting Stuart to write his wife, "The ladies of Maryland make a great fuss over your husband—loading me with bouquets—begging for autographs, buttons, etc. What shall I do?"[105] The cavalier was clearly in his element.

The war once again turned deadly, though, as the Antietam (or Sharpsburg) campaign intensified. After screening out prying Union scouts and scouting himself, he and his troops endured the bloodiest single day of the Civil War (September 17, 1862). They anchored the Rebels' left flank with his horse artillery. They also

Dead Confederate soldiers lie on the field in preparation for burial after the battle at Antietam. Stuart and his cavalry were able to hold a crumbling flank at Antietam until reinforcements arrived.

patched holes in Lee's crumbling lines with all the stragglers and rear area noncombatants that they could round up. Thus repaired, the lines managed to hold long enough for last-minute reinforcements to arrive on the field and end the fighting on a stalemate. The battered but unbeaten Army of Northern Virginia withdrew from Maryland two days later, with the potential for invading the North at another date.

Bloodless Glory

Stuart, however, was not quite through with the Yankees in Maryland. Three weeks after the fighting at Sharpsburg, he took twelve hundred troopers and rode another embarrassing loop around George McClellan and his men. This time, he raced before them up to Chambersburg, Pennsylvania, and slashed back down through their rear between Washington and Frederick, Maryland. He crossed the Potomac into the safety of Virginia after two furious days of chases, pursuits, escapes, and skirmishes with only one casualty to report. One of his riders said, "He rode with his advance guard, and was ever ready to seize and improve any opportunity. He trusted in Providence with an honest and sincere faith: but he also kept his powder dry." [106]

The newspapers spread their jubilation over the Chambersburg raid throughout the Confederacy and buoyed the Southern people's hopes once again. The writers reveled in Stuart's appropriation of twelve hundred badly needed horses, the capture of important civilians to be traded for Confederate men, and the wealth of intelligence he brought back related to the strength, position, and intentions of the Union army. As far as the newspapers were concerned, the flamboyant Stuart could ride rings around the stumbling Yankees without harm and, sadly, he began to believe his own press clippings.

Understandably, the continued ease of his exploits and the glory that the Southern people heaped upon him were beginning to infuse him with a dangerous sense of overconfidence. Although he prayed daily, he apparently neglected to review a biblical admonition which might have saved him from approaching disaster. "Pride goeth before destruction," Proverbs 16:18 warned, "and a haughty spirit before a fall."

From Corps Command to Embarrassing Portent

General Stuart spent the following winter at Lee and Jackson's sides, performing all the support duties required of the mounted arm and partying nightly with a band his banjo player, Sweeney,

Stuart was able to forget his grief over the death of his daughter during the intense fighting at Chancellorsville, where Stuart took over for the mortally wounded Stonewall Jackson.

had thrown together. The gaiety ended for Stuart, though, when Flora telegraphed him that little Flora had died suddenly of a fever. The grief devastated him for months and would have continued longer had the winter lull not ended at Chancellorsville in central Virginia, where he forgot himself in the intensity of combat.

In that horror, perhaps the most dynamic Confederate victory of the war, Jeb distinguished himself at the head of several cavalry charges, even taking over temporarily for the mighty Stonewall when Rebels accidentally shot him. A fellow general said of Stuart's impromptu assumption of corps command during the fog of battle,

> Altogether, I do not think there was a more brilliant thing done in the war than Stuart's extricating that command from the extremely critical position in which he found it as promptly and as boldly as he did. His attack never stopped to draw its breath until it had crashed through everything and our forces stood united around Chancellor's House [the Union headquarters].[107]

Stuart did cause one near calamity not long after that at Brandy Station, Virginia, in June 1863. There, his overconfidence began to weaken his judgment and he allowed ten thousand Union cavalrymen to surprise attack his nine thousand troopers while they were parading about like peacocks, staging play-fights for the benefit of some Confederate politicians and their tittering belles. The actual fighting that exploded onto the fields lasted a full day and mushroomed into the largest cavalry battle on the North American continent. The Rebel troopers, with severe casualties, barely managed to fend off the Yankees, but Stuart had definitely been caught with his boots off and that tarnished his reputation considerably.

Gettysburg Claims Another Reputation

Eager to regain his good name, Stuart practically begged General Lee to let him attempt a third ride around the Union army, this one to link up with Lee on his upcoming second invasion of the North. Lee agreed but only with the clear understanding that Stuart return in time to serve as his eyes and ears as he groped his way toward a winner-take-all show in Pennsylvania.

Problems befell Stuart at once, however. He discovered that the shorter loop he had planned to take around the Yankees was cut off, forcing him to swing much wider east to get around the mammoth Union army. Muddy roads and the burden of captured prisoners and wagons further slowed down the Confederate horsemen.

Hospital tents line the countryside of Gettysburg after the battle. Lee blamed Stuart's tardy arrival for the Confederacy's loss of thousands of men during the battle.

The delay was critical. General Stuart did not make it back to Lee until late on July 2, the eve of the third and final day of the Battle of Gettysburg and, by that time, the lack of intelligence on the Union army had already contributed sorely to the Confederate army's losses. On that last day, Stuart fought the Yankee cavalry gallantly but without appreciable results. He also covered Lee's retreat from Pennsylvania courageously but it was a retreat nonetheless and his name began to figure prominently among those responsible for it.

One of his most loyal officers even remarked, "It was the absence of Stuart that General Lee felt most keenly; for on him he had learned to rely to such an extent that it seemed as if his cavalry were concentrated in his person, and from him alone could information be expected." [108] Stuart would spend the remaining months of his life trying to deflect the many criticisms leveled against him for the reversal of Southern fortunes that followed the Battle of Gettysburg. That pivotal struggle had darkened yet another Confederate career in addition to any hopes the Army of Northern Virginia had for waging offensive warfare. And ominously, Jeb's banjo player, Sweeney, died shortly thereafter of pneumonia, eliminating the sing-alongs that had long lightened General Stuart's campfires.

The Fangs of a Cornered Beast

The Confederate army did not lie down and crawl away after the loss at Gettysburg. Two more years remained until its end at Appomattox Court House. Every battle afterward, though, had to be fought defensively and with dwindling resources in an effort to protect Richmond from collapse. The most gruesome of these battles occurred at the Wilderness and Spotsylvania Court House.

Between increasingly close scrapes with death, Jeb still managed to find enough free time to write to Flora. His letters hummed with even greater poignancy, that is, a sweet sadness, because she was pregnant with their third child. Once born, Jeb named their new daughter Virginia Pelham Stuart in honor of his "country" and a cherished friend who had fallen in battle a few months earlier. He also managed to slip down to Richmond during the ball season to brag about his "Miss Virginia" and swirl with the belles.

Back at the front, he kept up the crafty magic that had earned him his fame. He stalled the advance of a colossal Union force for a critical night by having his troops light enough campfires for an entire Confederate division. He then enhanced the ruse by racing his one regimental band back and forth through the fire-lit expanse,

A Confederate soldier lies dead after the battle of Spotsylvania. Stuart's tactics helped divert Union troops from attacking Lee's rear during the conflict.

making the music of many phantom musicians. The magic worked and the Yankees balked, buying General Lee enough time to reinforce the position.

But nothing could stop the blue hordes that trampled through the scrub growth and burning trees at the Wilderness, although Stuart helped to divert them around the Rebel right flank. Then he thundered ahead of the Confederate infantry and prevented the advance Yankee force from attacking Lee's rear at Spotsylvania Court House. The resulting Battle of Spotsylvania included the longest and most vicious hand-to-hand combat of the war but served to deflect the Unionists into more time-consuming fighting. Stuart again drove his cavalrymen ahead to counter the next expected Yankee thrust but the Unionists were as fatigued as the Confederates from ten days of steady fighting and both sides settled in for what amounted to a day off.

God's Will Be Done

Jeb enjoyed the brief lull that followed, especially since Flora visited him in camp and brought along Jemmie and Miss Virginia. General Lee even made a special trip to see the baby girl, and Jemmie, now five, gleefully rampaged among the troopers.

The peace did not hold, though. On May 9, Yankee cavalry began to move on Richmond and Flora had to flee with the children. On the road to cut off the enemy, Jeb could not help snatching a few more precious moments with his family. He did not even have time to dismount when he reached the house where they were staying. He could only bend down from his saddle and hug them all as if he might never see them again.

Stuart then galloped to an obscure crossroads known locally as Yellow Tavern just in time to place his men between Richmond and twelve thousand attacking Yankee cavalrymen. He managed to rally his scarecrow riders and repulse the initial avalanche of blue coats, slashing and shooting them back to their lines. In the middle of this battle, he did not see a dismounted Unionist beneath him nor hear his own men shrieking to alert him. It is doubtful he even heard the point-blank carbine shot that blew him from his saddle and lodged a bullet deep into his gut.

Last Words and Unspoken Farewells

Jeb Stuart had always been a garrulous talker and, even mortally wounded, he remained true to form. When an aide rushed to his side, he ordered, "Leave me, Dorsey, and go back to your men and fight." Dorsey disobeyed and dragged his commander back to an ambulance. His second in command leaped down from his horse but Stuart pushed him away and urged, "You are in command now. Go ahead, old fellow. I know you will do what's right." [109]

From the rickety wagon, he saw some of his troopers begin to retreat and he shouted, "Go back! Go back and do your duty as I have done mine. I'd rather die than be whipped!" They heard his call and rallied in time to halt the advancing Unionists. Finally, he allowed the springless ambulance to jolt him toward the rear. The jostling accelerated the bleeding from his wound. A lieutenant attempted to comfort him by saying that he looked well and would be all right. Stuart replied, "Well, I don't know how this will turn out; but if it is God's will that I shall die I am ready." [110]

The general's entourage took him to his brother-in-law's house where a doctor tried to administer a medicinal dose of whiskey. Stuart resisted because of the childhood vow he had made his mother (although one of his staff managed to coax it down).

Throughout the night and into the next day Stuart clung tenaciously to an ever-thinning thread of life. He hovered just above consciousness but he managed to accomplish much during his dimming moments.

Jeb stated that he wanted his personal effects sent to Flora and bequeathed his two magnificent horses to officers he favored. He left his gold spurs to the widow of an old comrade and gave his

saber to Jemmie, his rambunctious little boy. President Jefferson Davis rode up from Richmond, the city for which Jeb had taken a bullet to save, and asked him how he felt. Stuart answered, "Easy, sir, but willing to die if God and my country think I have fulfilled my destiny and done my duty." [111]

He sang "Rock of Ages" with a chaplain his aides had summoned but he did so with a wispy voice. He asked for Flora over and over but the doctor told him that she would probably not arrive in time. "I am resigned," he whispered, "if it be God's will; but I would like to see my wife. But God's will be

James Ewell Brown Stuart died as a result of a gunshot wound he received during a battle in 1864.

done." [112] And then he died a full day after having been wounded.

When the bad news reached Robert E. Lee, he paid the young cavalier what was, to him, the greatest compliment he could offer a cavalryman. "He never brought me a piece of false information," he said. "I can scarcely think of him without weeping." [113] Flora and her children poured their tears into skirts and strong arms when they arrived three hours after his death. Likewise, millions of Southerners sank into despair over the loss of their most hope-inspiring general.

Legacy and Lunacy

As untimely as Jeb Stuart's death seemed to those who loved him, it is something of a miracle that he lived as long as he did (thirty-one years). He had always been drawn to danger like a vine to the scorching sun. From his childhood assault on a hornets' nest to his bloody-nosed fights at West Point, he appeared to be apprenticing for a violent craft. His single-warrior combat with western Indians and outlaws introduced him to battle and he found he liked it.

During the Civil War, he strolled through battlefields of his own creation and dashed around and through entire armies. He led from the front without a thought for his own safety, enthusing his men by his calm recklessness. As if actually protected by the God in whom he trusted, bullets pierced nothing more than his coat and silk-lined cape. Many of his horses toppled with lead meant for him and shells that beheaded those around him only left a stinging ring in his ears.

But Jeb's "divine protection" ran out at about the same time as the Confederacy's and they came under historians' scrutiny in tandem. Ardent Southerners, convinced of the perfection of their "lost cause," had to look for some fallible human to blame for its demise. Since Gettysburg had been the turning point of the war and since Jeb Stuart (among others) had made critical errors there, it only followed in the minds of some staunch Confederates and some near-lunatics that he should take the blame for losing the entire war.

For many years the name Stuart was tarnished in the South due to the Happy Cavalier's mistakes at Gettysburg. Many speeches, letters to the editor, and memoirs of those who served with him eventually polished that name again. And what a name it was, Major General James Ewell Brown Stuart, and what a life it conjured: one so adventuresome, free-spirited, violent, and honorable that it remains synonymous with the cavalier spirit of the Old South.

CHAPTER 6

Nathan Bedford Forrest: The Best and the Worst

On April 7, 1862, General Nathan Bedford Forrest sat tall in his saddle, all six feet, two inches of hard body, chiseled face, and devilish goatee. At Pittsburg Landing, Tennessee, his tight-cinched eyes studied the approach of some 2,000 perfectly aligned Union soldiers splashing their way through boggy water and over a jumble of fallen timbers. Just behind him on the low ridge overlooking the bog was a hodge-podge of less than 350 Rebel cavalrymen. All of them looked gaunt and pale following the past two days of fighting the Battle of Shiloh. But their granite expressions indicated that they still had at least one fight left in them this day.

The battle was over now, at least the worst of it, and Forrest had the job of protecting the rear of the Confederate withdrawal. His commanders expected nothing more of him than to slow down the pursuing Yankees with sniper fire and, perhaps, a few ambushes on their flanks. But Bedford Forrest took every opportunity to inflict maximum casualties upon the enemy. After all, he had always said in his frontier twang, "war means fightin' and fightin' means killin'." [114]

His eyes flared when he saw just such an opportunity reveal itself. The broken ground over which the Union men were struggling was causing uneven gaps to open up in their lines and Forrest wasted no time in exploiting them. Waving his saber over his head, he yelled to his troops to charge. And his band of tired troopers exploded to new life, bounding down the slope after their general.

The Rebel horsemen burst upon the shocked Yankees in an avalanche of horse and steel. Forrest, still in the lead, cut his way through the Yankee's first line, second line, and well into the third before realizing that he had gone too far. His men had already turned and gotten away with their lives and he swore to do the same. A hive of swarming Yankees cried, "Kill him! Kill the goddam rebel! Knock him off his horse!" [115] Forrest flashed rabidly and hacked his saber into the seething mob. He cut off fingers, ears, and the better part of faces, plunging the blade through hearts and lungs and guts, until one brave Yankee rushed in close enough to jam the muzzle of his rifle flush against him and blow a ball of burning lead into his side.

The blast lifted Forrest out of the saddle but he managed to maintain control of his horse. He spurred the wounded animal to a leap and bolted away amid a hurricane of bullets. Forrest knew he needed quick cover to avoid being hit again so he jerked an unlucky Yankee boy up behind him in the saddle, and allowed him to absorb the deadly fusillade.

Safely out of rifle range, Forrest dropped his human shield and galloped back to the ridge from which he had come. His troopers gathered around him in dumbfounded disbelief and eased him from the saddle. Grimacing and weak, Forrest had but one question to ask. "Did we stop the Yankees?" He had to know. And the answer was a jubilant "Yes!"[116] Satisfied with the result, he let them carry him from the field to the doctors, where the rest of his ordeal began.

Doctors told him that the bullet was lodged against his spine and that the surgery to remove it might paralyze him. Refusing the

The Confederates attack the Union at the battle of Shiloh. Nathan Bedford Forrest's miraculous performance at this battle—which included receiving a bullet to the spine and riding a wounded horse to safety— earned him a legendary reputation.

operation for a matter of weeks, he finally submitted to the surgeon's blade when he saw himself getting no better. And he did so without any anesthesia. Just two weeks later, the "Wizard of the Saddle," as he became known, was riding again in search of more Yankees to kill.

The story of Nathan Bedford Forrest at Shiloh spread through the newspapers, North and South, adding to his fame for good or ill. More and more people wanted to know, "Who is this man, this uneducated backwoodsman? Is he a heathen or a hero? And what was it that made him such a killer?"

Never Much of a Child

Nathan Bedford Forrest was born in the sweltering, bug-infested humidity of his parents' dirt-floored log cabin. The date was July 13, 1821; the place, the backwoods of western Tennessee. Other great men had begun this way: Davy Crockett, Andrew Jackson, and even his ultimate archenemy, Abraham Lincoln, but none of them had absorbed the frontier's brutal lessons quite as thoroughly as Forrest.

Death equated with life to young Bedford, in both positive and negative ways. By the age of five he was helping with slain deer and butchered hogs, catching and gutting fish, and remorselessly exterminating any and all creatures that threatened the crops. Even nature's nurturing rains took lives when, every spring, they turned to fatal floods up and down the Mississippi River valley. In the backwoods, death and violence were simply a basic condition of people's lives, rich and poor, free and slave. Bedford learned that harsh lesson early.

He also learned that death and violence often had little redeeming value, particularly when they took the form of rattlesnake bites and panther claws, blizzards and earthquakes, and the most dreaded of all calamities, disease. Typhus killed three of his sisters and two of his brothers in one unfeeling scourge. He barely survived the fevers himself. However, he suffered his most grievous loss when, after the family moved from Tennessee to an equally desolate part of Mississippi, his beloved father died, at least in part from the constant rigors of trying and, in large part, failing to keep his family alive.

Bedford, now sixteen and the oldest remaining child, had to take over where his father had left off, providing food, clothing, security, and discipline to his three younger brothers. He later recalled that he "would labor all day in the field and then sit up at night and work until it was late making buckskin leggings and shoes and coon-skin caps for his younger brothers."[117] His mother did what she could to provide for the family but the man-boy Forrest found himself the head of the homestead whether he wanted the responsibility or not. And he immediately set to work to ensure that neither he nor any of his kin would ever have to pass from this earth as poor and broken as his father.

Student of Life/Teacher of Lessons

Bedford Forrest never had much time for schooling and, when he did attend, he only excelled at recess. One of his former teachers said, "Bedford had plenty of sense, but would not apply himself. He thought more of wrestling than his books; he was an athelete." And he was usually at the head of his class when it came to getting punished. The semiliterate General Forrest later remarked, "I never see a pen what I don't think of a snake."[118]

Young Bedford considered shooting, tracking, and horseback riding as lessons worth studying and he learned them well. Once he and his mother were riding home from a visit with friends when a panther leaped from a tree and attacked the woman's shoulders and back. Bedford grappled with the shrieking cat and knocked it to the ground where it fled into the trackless woods. He shepherded his bleeding mother home to be cared for by his little brothers and then set out with his dogs.

The dogs treed the beast after a full day of tracking. They yelped all night while Bedford, his skin shredded by thorns and brambles, waited for enough light to get off a shot. He willed himself awake, taunted by visions of only wounding the big cat with his single-shot rifle. He knew too well the damage a bloodied pan-

Forrest's legendary bravery was earned at a young age when he tracked and killed a panther that had attacked his mother.

ther could inflict. As the night began giving way to the dawn, a silhouette appeared in the tree. The panther was creeping down the trunk. It hissed to keep the dogs at bay and suddenly sprang toward the bush where Bedford was crouching.

In an oozing, endless second, Bedford raised his rifle, aimed down the barrel, and blasted away. The smoke rushed and billowed, preventing him from seeing whether or not he had hit the animal, but at last he could make out the form of the creature lying dead at his feet. He slashed off its ears to confirm the kill and headed for home, too fatigued and shock-worn to revel in the glory.

Other Game

Guns and confrontations had long been an integral part of every-day life for Bedford as they had been for all men on the frontier. He shot and killed a neighbor's prize ox and nearly shot the neighbor after the lumbering animal repeatedly crashed through his fence and thrashed the cornfield that fed his family. Adopting Andrew Jackson's maxim "Take time to deliberate, but when the time for action arrives, stop thinking," [119] Bedford found himself prone to quick and sometimes rash action.

At his death, one newpaperman would later write, "He was simply one of those men who considered himself bound to avenge an insult on the instant it was given, and a man so arbitrary and determined as Forrest was certain to provoke insults." [120] Bedford had already been involved in gunfights, knifefights, and innumerable fistfights by his early twenties. In some, he had killed, in most, he had merely wounded, but in all, an injury to his pride had provoked him to violence. It would take a little more age, a few white-collar business opportunities, and a wife to soothe a little of the savage in Nathan Bedford Forrest, and even then he would not be a man with whom to be trifled.

Horse Trader, Husband, and Big Farmer

As a youth, Bedford had taken a trip to Texas, where he saw his first real plantations. Their power, grace, and grandeur planted within him the dream of someday owning his own. Those who did not know Forrest well discouraged him, saying that he was destined to follow in his father's, grandfather's, and great-grandfather's paths, working hard, staying poor, and dying young. It was the Forrest way, the frontier way. But Bedford refused to let that dream die and he began looking for ways to fan it into flames.

Bedford's confidence, charisma, and unflinching willingness to "take down" armed drunkards and bullies already had people calling him a "local hero," an "honorable man," and "more of a sheriff than the one we've got." [121] They showed their respect by electing him coroner and lieutenant of the militia company. Such stature in the community could not go unnoticed for long and a well-known horse trader in the area capitalized upon it. Bedford became the man's partner and began "acquiring year after year a more comfortable future." [122] Always frugal (in all things except gambling), he saved his money and invested in land. He had soon amassed enough acreage to carve out a sprawling farm for his mother, stepfather, and brothers. All he needed now was a wife so he could start a family of his own.

In typical Bedford Forrest fashion, he chose the young woman he wanted to marry, pursued her relentlessly, and asked for her hand without a doubt that he would win. Her name was Mary Ann Montgomery and he met her when rescuing her carriage from a swollen river. Two other suitors watched from the bank, laughing at the girl's predicament. When Bedford got Mary Ann safely back to her house, he beat both the young men for their poor showing and forbade them from ever appearing on Mary Ann's doorstep again. They did not. The only obstacle left to clear from his path was the girl's father who resisted the union, saying, "Why, Bedford, I couldn't consent. And while you don't drink, you cuss and gamble and Mary Ann is a Christian girl." Forrest overcame the argument, replying, "I know it, sir, and that's just why I want her!" [123] Three weeks later, she was his.

From Slave Owner to Slave Seller

By 1850, Forrest had a son and a daughter, a stage coach line, a brickyard, and three slaves. He realized, while negotiating for the latter, that buying and selling slaves was practically the same as buying and selling horses. He thus moved to Memphis and hung out a shingle as a slave trader. His salesmanship skills soon made him a millionaire, well known and admired throughout the teeming city. Always a man of his time and place, Bedford had no qualms whatsoever about treating human beings like so much horseflesh. And he was careful to treat the black humans in his inventory as well as he had always treated his finest horses.

While his concern for the well-being of the slaves was solely based upon his commitment to provide quality workers to buyers, it was nonetheless laudable that, according to one of his advertisements, his "regulations [were] exact and systematic, cleanliness, neatness and comfort being strictly observed and enforced. [His] aim [was] to furnish to customers A.1 servants, and field hands, sound and perfect to customers." [124] And he was also acknowledged as a trader who kept black families together whenever possible.

With his accumulating wealth, Forrest finally bought the plantation of which he had dreamed since his youth. It was, according to a legal document "a splendid plantation in Coahoma County,

Mississippi, with two hundred field hands, and making upwards of 1,000 bales of cotton yearly." [125] But even the gentility that supposedly accompanied plantation life couldn't tame Bedford Forrest. In a business transaction that revealed an associate's duplicity, Forrest was heard to blaze,

> You infernal scoundrel! Do you dare ask me to be as damned a rascal as yourself? I have a big notion to pitch you in the Mississippi River! Now, I warn you if you ever presume to address such a damnable proposition to me in the future I will break your rascally neck! [126]

The questionable transaction was never attempted again by his associate, who thereafter always acknowledged his partner's towering rage.

An Outlet for That Rage

Bedford Forrest was thirty-nine years old in 1860 and he had already accomplished every goal that he had ever set for himself. There was every reason to assume that he could live out the rest of his life in peace and prosperity. But then South Carolina seceded from the Union, making the long-feared civil war appear imminent. And when his home state of Tennessee threw its fortunes in with the fledgling Confederacy, he felt he had no other choice but to enlist.

Forrest had no formal military training nor friends within the closed fraternity of professional army officers to assist him in getting a commission, so he settled for the rank of private in a mounted rifle regiment. Before long, though, a few political friends in Memphis brought his leadership skills to light and went to work to get him a commission. One petitioned the governor, referring to himself as one "knowing Forrest well and having a high regard for the man." [127] The influence worked and Forrest was soon a colonel with orders to raise his own cavalry regiment.

His recruiting posters aptly reflected his view of the war:

> 200 ABLE-BODIED MEN WANTED BY THE FIRST OF JUNE WITH GOOD HORSE AND GUN. I WISH NONE BUT THOSE DESIRING TO BE ACTIVELY ENGAGED. COME ON, BOYS, IF YOU WANT TO HAVE A HEAP OF FUN AND TO KILL SOME YANKEES! [128]

Forrest signed up far more men than the newborn Confederate army could equip and he ended up paying for their horses, guns, uniforms, and supplies out of his own pocket. He was worth a million and a half dollars by that time but the expense was still quite high. It quickly prepared his troopers for battle, though, and he led them out of Memphis salivating for their first fight.

A Freezing Ride and a Bloody Side

Colonel Forrest broke in his enthusiastic but inexperienced troopers during a far-flung, six-month campaign consisting of miscellaneous raids and skirmishes in Kentucky and Tennessee, which ended up at Fort Donelson, a set of earthen artillery emplacements and breastworks guarding the Cumberland River approaches to the deep South. From February 13 to 16, 1862, the Rebel army took a pounding from Union naval and infantry troops during a miserable storm of sleet, snow, and icy rain. Poor leadership on the part of the Southern generals led to the surrender of the hard-fighting Confederate soldiers but Forrest refused to turn over his men to the Unionists when they still had fight left in them. Instead, he went to his shivering men and announced, "Boys, these people are talking about surrendering, and I am going out of this place before they do or bust hell wide open!" [129] And the riders followed him from Fort Donelson along a road flooded with ice-encrusted water chest deep to their horses and knee deep to themselves.

Union forces at Fort Donelson capture Confederate troops in 1862. Forrest refused to give up his men, escaping through a flooded road to fight another day.

The Battle of Shiloh came next, at the end of which he and his men covered the withdrawal of the Confederate army. It was there that he single-handedly battled the pursuing Yankees and took a bullet in his spine. He considered the cost worth the result, though, when he heard the Union commander's reaction: "The enemy's cavalry came down boldly at a charge, led by Forrest in person, breaking through our line of skirmishers; when the regiment of infantry, broke, threw away their rifles, and fled." [130]

The Best and Worst Rear Their Heads

Forrest decided, after being attached to large Confederate forces at Fort Donelson and Shiloh, that he preferred the independent command of a smaller unit (between fifteen hundred and two thousand riders). It fit his personality to answer to no one but himself and the tactics he employed were best suited for less cumbersome bodies of men. After surrounding a Yankee garrison in July 1862 at Murfreesboro, Tennessee, and taking a few prisoners, Forrest's lieutenants advised him that they were outnumbered and should disengage. He fired back, "I did not come here to make half a job of it! I mean to have them all!" [131] Yet he baffled his officers by disengaging his troopers and sending them on a continuous ride around the town.

He then strutted down the main street under a white flag and called for a truce, demanding of the Union commander, "Surrender unconditionally or I will have every man put to the sword!" His troopers were now cantering their horses up and down the streets, "showing more men than I actually had." [132] Forrest's ploy worked, enhanced as it no doubt was by his growing reputation as a commander who carried out his threats. He took more Union prisoners than he had men in his own command, including many blacks. His personal handling of at least two of them appeared to have set the tone for how he intended to treat "damned nigger soldiers" [133] for the rest of the war.

One Southern trooper captured a black man dressed in federal blue and turned him over to Forrest. The Confederate said,

> I soon found General Forrest sitting on his horse his eyes blazing fire. Instead of complimenting me for recovering a fine big buck Negro, he gave me a cussing, saying that a dead nigger in Federal uniform was more valuable to the Confederacy than a live one. [134]

Another Rebel claimed that when a "mulatto man, who was the servant to one of the officers in the Union forces, was brought to Forrest, the General deliberately put his hand to his holster, drew a pistol, and blew the man's brains out." [135]

Whether these incidents actually occurred as the observers stated is a historical uncertainty. Other relevant aspects are verifiable, however. Nathan Bedford Forrest was a slave owner and a slave seller. He, like most other Southerners of the old order, had never seen a slave read, write, or speak in such a way as to indicate intelligent thought because, of course, they had been denied the opportunity to learn such skills. Nevertheless, Forrest did not consider the black man to be the equal of the white under any circumstances and, consequently, he felt no need to treat black prisoners of war with the same decency that he did white ones (as long as the whites were not so-called traitors from Tennessee who joined). At any rate, it was at Murfreesboro, Tennessee, in the summer of 1862 that Nathan Bedford Forrest unequivocally let his sentiments be known regarding the fighting black man.

Losing with Style

Throughout the fall and winter of 1862, Bedford Forrest conducted a series of hassling raids in western Tennessee against Union general Ulysses S. Grant. A man who knew Grant well said of his reaction to Forrest,

> He was the only Confederate cavalryman of whom Grant stood in much dread. If Forrest was in command he at once became apprehensive, because the latter was amenable to no known rules of procedure, was a law unto himself for all military acts, and was constantly doing the unexpected at all times and places.[136]

In his lightning campaign, Forrest employed a collection of tricks to fool the enemy into thinking that he commanded more men than he actually did. One of his artillerymen reported,

> No device for creating this impression was too insignificant to be called into play. The constant beating of kettle drums, the lighting and tending of numerous fires, moving pieces of artillery from one point to another, the dismounting of cavalry and parading them as infantry—nothing was overlooked.[137]

At Parker's Crossroad, Tennessee, on December 31, he employed all of these techniques as well as other Forrest favorites such as double flanking envelopments (or getting around both ends of the enemy's line), cannister-filled artillery pieces (ordnance consisting of hundreds of rifle balls) pushed into the enemies' faces, and dismounted cavalrymen advancing from rock to tree to bush like Indians. As a result, he had the numerically superior Yankees on the run. Complete victory appeared imminent until the frozen woods behind him and his men erupted in gunfire and hordes of enemy infantry came crashing down upon their rear.

Caught in the very type of trap that he himself had sprung on his enemies many times before, Forrest hustled together all the couriers that he could and sent them galloping off to his spread-out troops with one desperate order: "Charge them both ways!" [138] The Rebel troopers closest to the front bowled over the weakened Yankees and burst to freedom beyond them. Forrest led the remainder in a headlong frenzy in reverse and they fought their way out. He lost many men to capture and death but he managed to remove the bulk of them to safety. And as if to inform the Unionists that his losses were not as devastating as they might have hoped, Forrest led a successful raid against them the very next day. He knew he had been fooled, though, at Parker's Crossroad, and he determined that such an embarrassing and costly slip-up would never happen again.

The Price of Courage

Between February and May 1863, Forrest swung from one extreme to the other. On the downswing, he attempted to take old Fort Donelson, at Dover, Tennessee (from which he and his men had barely escaped capture a year earlier). Forrest's impetuous courage got him in trouble this time. He insisted on a mounted frontal assault when he mistakenly thought the Yankees were abandoning the earthworks. But they were not fleeing. They were rushing to man their cannons and the Union commander recorded part of the result. "In an instant," he wrote, "the siege gun was double-shotted with cannister, and turned upon them and discharged, tearing one man to atoms and two horses, within ten feet of the muzzle." [139]

Forrest himself had two horses shot from beneath him and he barely got away with his life. Almost a thousand other Confederates were not so lucky. In another expression of his dark side, Forrest blamed the disaster on the overall commander of the operation, hissing at him, "I will be in my coffin before I will fight again under your command." [140] And he rode off with his survivors.

Locks and Lies

On the upswing of his spring 1863 campaign, Forrest relentlessly dogged a Union cavalry foray into Alabama led by the luckless Abel D. Streight. Streight had seventeen hundred men while Forrest's troopers, still depleted from their defeat at Fort Donelson,

General Forrest leads his men in a frontal assault at Dover, Tennessee, which resulted in the death of almost a thousand soldiers under his command.

amounted to only four hundred. After a few weeks of skirmishes, Forrest managed to chase Streight's men across the better part of the deep South, leaving the Yankees little time to destroy railroads and plantations as they had been ordered.

Nipping at the heels of the Unionists, Forrest ordered that "whenever you see anything blue, shoot at it, and do all you can to keep up the scare" and "devil them all day and all night." [141] The Yankees were plenty scared and plenty deviled by the time they reached the Alabama-Georgia border and, more important, they were utterly exhausted by the Rebels' twenty-four-hour harassment.

Forrest had avoided fatiguing his own men by having them operate in two shifts, one raiding while the other slept, thereby "keeping up the scare" and keeping half his men rested at the same time. The result was inevitable. When the Yankees finally collapsed and had to put up a fight, Streight reported, "A large portion of my best troops actually went to sleep while lying in line of battle under a severe skirmish fire." [142]

All that separated Forrest from his sleepy quarry was a river, the bridge over which the Yankees had burned. Never one to be stopped by a mere body of water, he searched out the nearest cabin and found a sixteen-year-old girl named Emma Sansom who said she knew of a nearby ford and would lead him to it. He pulled her up on the back of his horse just as the girl's mother came rushing to her rescue. Forrest tipped his hat to the older woman and reassured her, "Don't be uneasy ma'am. I will bring her back safe." [143] And he did, trading her a personal note of thanks for a lock of her hair. Forrest's men then forded the river and aligned for battle.

Forrest approached the Yankee Streight under a white flag and demanded his surrender, claiming that he had three thousand Rebel troopers behind him in the woods. He reinforced this ruse by having his few troopers ride in a seamless circle in and out of the trees to his rear. He also ordered up couriers and sent them galloping off with urgent commands to nonexistent regiments and artillery batteries to give the enemy the impression that he had more men than he actually had. With a poker master's face, he then told Colonel Streight, "I've got enough men to whip you out of your boots." [144]

Unnerved, Streight succumbed to the ploy, surrendering his force of seventeen hundred men to Forrest's four hundred. Forrest later wrote, "When Streight saw we were barely four hundred, he did rear! He demanded to have his arms back and that we should fight it out. I just laughed and patted him on the shoulder, and said 'Ah, Colonel, all is fair in love and war you know!'" [145]

The Enemy Within

Perhaps Bedford Forrest's most intense battle of the war came not when confronted by Northerners but when attacked face-to-face by one of his own officers, a young horse artillery lieutenant by the name of A. W. Gould. Forrest had severely reprimanded Gould for allowing two of his big guns to be captured during the campaign against Colonel Streight, viciously calling Gould's honor and courage into question.

After brooding and sulking for several days, Lieutenant Gould tracked his commander down in Columbia, Tennessee, with the intention of shooting him dead. He found Forrest in Columbia's Masonic Hall fiddling with a closed penknife. Trembling, Gould tried to justify his impending murder with a speech on the necessity of defending one's name and reputation. Forrest replied in kind but with pure, fearless anger.

He shouted into Gould's face, again calling him a coward and a liar. Gould could only stammer over and over, "It's false! That's all false!" [146] The two lunged at each other, Gould firing a pistol hidden in his trouser pocket and Forrest stabbing with the penknife he had managed to open with his teeth. Each inflicted serious wounds upon the other before enough men could arrive to pull them apart.

Gould stumbled from the building, clutching his bleeding side. Forrest grimaced at the pain of the pistol ball in his hip, his voice thundering after him, "No damned man shall kill me and live!" [147] Gould did not live, perishing from his injuries later that day, but Nathan Bedford Forrest survived to fall into the trap that his time, place, and character had long since laid for him.

Justifications for the Unjust

The nature of the war had changed radically since the glory days of 1861. It had been corroded by three years of bloodshed and ever-diminishing respect for human life. By 1864, any lingering appearance of chivalry and fair play, parades and blushing maidens, was gone, replaced by the notions of total war that allowed little consideration for civilians or prisoners. Union general William T. Sherman's continuing pronouncements, "war is hell, it cannot be refined," "death is mercy," and "desolation follows our tracks," [148] set the tone for many Unionists under his command who waged war throughout the South, especially in the West where he served as the overall commander.

While Northern newspapers mentioned plenty of Southern improprieties, the unimpeachable *Official Records of the Union Army* later contained bountiful evidence of Yankee atrocities with which Forrest would have been acquainted. In his area of operations alone during 1863 and 1864, the *Official Records* admits to Union soldiers

"raping women white and colored, . . . burning civilian houses, . . . shooting to death civilian men without cause or provocation, . . . murdering prisoners or indulging those

115

who do, . . . inhumanly murdering and butchering 300 Rebel prisoners and leaving the half-dead to the mercy of brute creation, . . . robbing old negroes and debauching negro women, . . . shooting Negroes through the head," and hundreds of other similar incidents.[149]

Particularly galling to Confederate soldiers were depredations committed upon Southern whites, military and civilian, by the Northern "colored troops." The *Official Records* notes many of them, including

> "hanging prisoners without benefit of court-martial," "burning civilian houses and barns, eating up their livestock, and taking hostages from their families," "carrying away the families of guerrillas," "stealing, robbing, and maltreating women daily," "engaging in plundering forays," "insulting peaceful citizens and robbing them," "seizing civilians' wagons and filling them with furniture, tobacco, and such other property they desired," and "murdering white citizens." [150]

The *Official Records* reported on these atrocities, citing many more such abuses on the part of black troops and, added to the number carried out by white Yankees, Forrest's rage was bursting and about to deliver one of the most horrifying paybacks of the war.

Bayonets and Other Points of View

There is a Northern version and a Southern version of what transpired on April 12, 1864, at Fort Pillow, Tennessee, an earthen embattlement overlooking the Mississippi River some fifty miles north of Memphis. Both sides agreed that approximately fifteen hundred cavalrymen under General Nathan Bedford Forrest attacked the fort defended by about six hundred Federals, half black and half white. It took Forrest's men two assaults and several casualties to make it evident to the Yankees that the fort would fall. Forrest issued a surrender demand that included the cryptic words "should my demand be refused, I cannot be responsible for the fate of your command," [151] which the Union commander refused. Forrest's men then stormed the walls.

From there, accounts vary. Forrest reported,

> [Without surrendering], the enemy attempted to retreat to the river, either for protection of gunboats or to escape, and the slaughter was heavy. The river was dyed with the blood of the slaughtered for 200 yards. Many ran into the river and were drowned.

Another Southern witness recalled, "They refused to surrender, which incensed our men and if General Forrest had not run between our men and the Yanks with his pistol and saber drawn not a man would have been spared." [152]

Another Rebel remembered that when one of his officers shouted, "Kill the niggers!" a second countered, "No, Forrest says take them away and carry them with him to wait upon him and cook for him, and put them in jail to be returned to their masters," [153] a fate less than fair but perhaps more accommodating than death. A Confederate colonel said that, "General Forrest rode up on horseback and ordered me to go down the bluff and stop any and all firing by the Confederates at the retreating garrison. General Forrest was exceedingly anxious to check any undue slaughter." [154]

The Northerners disagreed with just about everything that the Southerners said. They believed the subsequent congressional report asserting that the Union garrison had fallen victim

> to the malignity and barbarity of Forrest and his followers;
> ... that the Rebels from the top on down had commenced an
> indiscriminate slaughter, sparing neither black or white, sol-
> dier or civilian, [and that] no cruelty which the most fiendish
> malignity could devise was omitted by these murderers.[155]

Battle rages at Fort Pillow as Forrest leads his men in bloody combat. Although it remains a matter of controversy, Forrest is said to have murdered the troops—which included blacks as well as whites—stationed at the fort.

Confederate troops take over the water batteries at Fort Pillow after defeating the Union troops there.

The political committee cited atrocities ranging from killing unarmed prisoners to burying blacks alive to burning tents containing their wounded.

One black soldier in the fort said,

> Our boys when they saw they were overpowered threw down their arms and held up handkerchiefs and some their hands in token of surrender, but no sooner were they seen than they were shot down and if one shot failed to kill them the bayonet or revolver did not.[156]

Another black reported that, after the Yankees surrendered, Forrest's men, "killed every negro that made his appearance dressed in Federal uniform; drunken rebel soldiers came up and fired in among the prisoners with their revolvers." [157]

Probably the most damning allegation against the conduct of General Forrest and his Confederates came from a Confederate who was present to see it.

> The poor deluded negros would run up to our men, fall upon their knees and with uplifted hands scream for mercy but they were shot down. Human blood stood about in pools and brains could have been gathered up in any quantity. Gen. Forrest ordered them shot down like dogs.[158]

Two Legacies

Regardless of which version of the events at Fort Pillow is closer to the truth, it cannot be denied that violent excesses took place. And it would appear that at least a few otherwise brave and self-less Southern patriots lost control of the aggression that fed their legitimate martial prowess. Out of control, they rampaged their way through some racially motivated killings. The numbers alone suggest that. The Southerners captured only fifty-eight of three hundred blacks while accepting the surrender of one hundred sixty-eight of three hundred whites.

But as always, the truth of what really occurred probably lies somewhere between the emotional versions put forth by the opposing sides, both of which had a prejudiced point of view from the start. And whether or not Bedford Forrest personally ordered, condoned, or participated in any atrocities matters little. He was in command of Southern forces at Fort Pillow and, as such, he must be held ultimately responsible for the mistreatment of any Union captives there.

And so he is today, whether justified or not. No matter how great or how numerous his military triumphs, the shadow of Fort Pillow still darkens his achievements in the eyes of his detractors. Even his signature victory at the Battle of Brice's Crossroad has been denied its full recognition among historians due to his loss of control over his Confederates at Fort Pillow. Military strategists, however, have long studied Forrest's deployments at Brice's Crossroad, that otherwise insignificant dot on the map where two dirt roads intersected in northern Mississippi. General George S. Patton and Field Marshal Erwin Rommel both studied his strategies in preparation for their blitzes in World War II and they are still required reading at military academies all over the globe.

Brice's Crossroad: The Setup

In June 1864, Union general William T. Sherman entered Georgia to "make her howl" [159] but he had one problem to deal with first: Nathan Bedford Forrest harrassing his supply lines to the rear. To eliminate the pesky Forrest once and for all time, Sherman ordered General Samuel D. Sturgis to track the Rebel down with five thousand infantrymen, three thousand cavalrymen, and twenty-two cannon. Forrest, with only forty-eight hundred troopers and far fewer artillery pieces, was still more than happy to give him the chance.

Forrest's scouts ascertained the route, direction, and speed of the Union advance, allowing him to choose ground that would be to his advantage in an ambush. He picked Brice's Crossroad because the Unionists would have to cross a narrow bridge to reach it, bottlenecking their troop movements, reinforcements, and supplies, and forcing the Yankees to arrive on the battlefield in driblets. The ground was also partially wooded and covered, which would prevent the Unionists from seeing just how few Confederates really faced them.

One of Bedford Forrest's favorite maxims of war was "Get there first with the most," [160] and while he almost never had the largest force in a battle, he almost always deployed those he had before his enemies could do so, and for good reason. By arriving on the field first, he could ensure that the troops advancing against him would have to march to get there on the day of the battle and exhaust themselves before they even had a chance to fight. And June 10, 1864, happened to dawn as the hottest, most humid day of the season, one, he knew, that would fatigue even the most seasoned of Union foot soldiers on their approach to the battlefield.

Employing another of his maxims, "Hit 'em on the end," [161] Forrest hid his troops in a horseshoe or semicircle around the crossroads so that when the first Unionists reached it, the Rebels would be positioned to strike not only the center of the Yankee lines but their right and left flanks as well. Forrest also deployed his artillery pieces far to the front (increasing the risk of their capture) so they could blast double loads of cannister into the enemy soldiers at point-blank range. And with that, the trap was set. The men were ready. All Forrest needed now were the Yankees to show up as predicted.

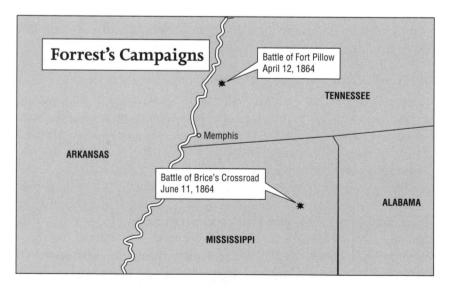

Brice's Crossroad: The Execution

In classic Bedford Forrest fashion, he had already articulated his entire plan before making a move. He had explained to his officers,

> The country is densely wooded and the undergrowth so heavy that when we strike them they will not know how few men we have. Their cavalry will move out ahead of the infantry, and should reach the crossroads three hours in advance. We can whip their cavalry in that time. As soon as the fight opens up, they will send back to have the infantry hurried up. It is going to be as hot as hell, and coming on a run for five or six miles over such roads, their infantry will be so tired out we will ride right over them.[162]

It was as if Forrest had read a crystal ball. The Union cavalry did arrive first, three thousand of the most rugged blue riders in the West. General Forrest ordered his men to dismount and "show fight [attack], a man in motion is worth two standing!"[163] He reported later, "We had a severe skirmish with the enemy, which was kept up until 1 o'clock, at which time [Confederate] General Buford arrived with more artillery, followed by [the last Confederate reinforcements]."[164]

After an hour's intense fighting, the Yankee horsemen sent back a desperate message to the infantry behind them. "Everything at the crossroads going to the devil as fast as it possibly can. The enemy is gaining ground, and the only thing that can save us is the infantry."[165] Then a pause in the action ensued, which Forrest wanted to break. Having stripped down to his billowy-sleeved shirt, he rode up and down his lines, shouting angrily at his men, "Get up! When you hear his guns, and the bugle sounds, every man must charge, and we will give them hell!" One of the Rebels recalled,

> Our movement was too slow to suit Forrest, he would curse, then praise, and then threaten to shoot us himself, if we were so afraid the Yanks might hit us. He would praise in one breath, then in the next would curse us until he finally said, "I will lead you." Then we hustled across that narrow field. It was a race.[166]

The Union cavalrymen fell back into their infantry who were arriving on the field but, as Forrest had predicted, the foot soldiers were too worn out to fight effectively. Many simply collapsed with heat exhaustion and awaited capture. More struggled to retreat across the narrow bridge over which they had just passed. Exploiting the Union confusion, Forrest rode to the right side of his semicircled lines and called in his unmistakable drawl, "Hit 'em on the e-e-end! Hit 'em on the e-e-end!" [167] And his right flank came crashing down on and behind the Unionists' left flank. This was too much for the Yankees to bear. The entire force broke and ran, throwing down their weapons to swim across the creek. Unsatisfied with the results, Forrest demanded that his men pursue and "keep up the skeer [scare]," [168] turning what remained of an orderly withdrawal into a complete and riotous rout.

Nightfall ended what perhaps had been, for the numbers involved, the most tightly conceived and executed Confederate victory of the Civil War. The statistics attested to as much. The Union suffered 2,300 casualties while the Rebels lost 400. In addition, Forrest's men captured 16 artillery pieces, 176 wagons, 1,500 rifles, and enough ammunition to fire them for the duration of the war. Nathan Bedford Forrest had struck again, securing his immortality in the South. His name would be remembered in the North as well but for entirely different reasons.

One War Ends, Another Never Does

The waning months of the Civil War saw Bedford Forrest and his men harrassing shipping along the Mississippi River, inhibiting the arrival of supplies to Unionists in the East, and conducting raids throughout the deep South that were too little and too late to do the dying Confederacy any good. At war's end, he was urged by many to wage a guerrilla campaign against the Union occupation forces overrunning the country but he declined, arguing that the South would fare best by submitting to Union authority. Musing that he had "gone into the army worth a million and a half dollars and come out a beggar," [169] he laid his sword down and returned to work peaceably as a planter and railroad official.

But when the Union garrison troops refused to adequately guard the Southern citizens from depredations committed by ex-slaves, Union deserters, and homeless whites, Forrest announced, "We have already lost all but our honor in the last war, and I must say, that in order to be men we must protect our honor at all hazards and we must also protect our wives, our homes, and our families." [170] He thus saw no other option but to throw his name and influence in with a newly formed secret organization dedicated to the protection of former Confederates and their families. The organization was called the Ku Klux Klan and he served as its first Grand Wizard for ten years.

By the mid-1870s, however, Forrest believed that the need for the Klan had diminished and that its methods had become too violent. He resigned and retired from public life, only to die in 1877 from injuries sustained from coming "out of the war pretty well wrecked, completely used up, shot to pieces, crippled up." [171]

The Unknown Soldier

For all the victories that Nathan Bedford Forrest legitimately won during the Civil War and all of his astounding feats of personal courage, his name never soared to the same heights as did those of Robert E. Lee, Stonewall Jackson, Jeb Stuart, or even James Longstreet. Perhaps, he surmised, that was because he operated in the Western theater,

A virulent racist, Forrest served as the Grand Wizard of the Ku Klux Klan for ten years after the Civil War. Here, an 1868 illustration depicts two Klan members dressed in full uniform.

far removed from the reporters and speech-makers of Richmond and Washington who made those in the East so famous.

But maybe, more to the point, it was that he was, as he himself conceded, "regarded in large communities at the North with abhorrence, as a detestable monster, ruthless and swift to take life." [172] He certainly knew that the winners of wars write the history books concerning them and that his association with the Fort Pillow massacre, the Ku Klux Klan, and the prewar slave trade would tarnish his reputation as a combat general. However, he must have also at least entertained the idea that, despite the dark side of his record, the name Nathan Bedford Forrest would surface again wherever military leadership, tactics, and personal fighting ability were esteemed. And, fortunately, for Southerners in need of heroes and Americans in need of military strategists, he would have been absolutely correct.

NOTES

Introduction: "The Man Is Everything"

1. Quoted in Gwynne Dyer, *War*. New York: Crown, 1985.

2. Quoted in David Chandler, *The Campaigns of Napoleon*. New York: Macmillan, 1966.

3. Quoted in Chandler, *The Campaigns of Napoleon*.

Chapter 1: Brothers of Different Mothers

4. Mary Boykin Chesnut, *A Diary from Dixie*. Cambridge, MA: Harvard University Press, 1980.

5. John A. Garraty, *The American Nation*. New York: Harper & Row, 1971.

6. Allen Nevins, quoted in Garraty, *The American Nation*.

7. David Donald, *The Civil War and Reconstruction*. Lexington, MA: Heath, 1969.

8. Quoted in Eric McKitirick, *Slavery Defended: The Views of the Old South*. Englewood, NJ: Prentice-Hall, 1963.

9. Quoted in Garraty, *The American Nation*.

Chapter 2: Robert E. Lee: More Man than Marble

10. Quoted in Douglas Southall Freeman, *Lee*. New York: Collier, 1993.

11. Quoted in Henry Steele Commager, *America's Robert E. Lee*. Lakeville, CT: Castle Press, 1991.

12. Quoted in Freeman, *Lee*.

13. Quoted in Clifford Dowdy, *Lee*. New York: Little, Brown, 1965.

14. Quoted in Freeman, *Lee*.

15. Quoted in Dowdy, *Lee*.

16. Quoted in Dowdy, *Lee*.

17. Quoted in Commager, *America's Robert E. Lee*.

18. Quoted in Freeman, *Lee*.

19. Quoted in Burke Davis, *Gray Fox: Robert E. Lee and the Civil War*. New York: Rinehart, 1956.

20. Quoted in Davis, *Gray Fox*.

21. Quoted in Gary W. Gallagher, ed., *Lee the Soldier*. Lincoln: University of Nebraska Press, 1996.

22. Quoted in Freeman, *Lee*.

23. Quoted in Gallagher, *Lee the Soldier*.

24. Quoted in Peter Earle, *Robert E. Lee*. New York: Saturday Review Press, 1974.

25. Quoted in Dowdy, *Lee*.

26. Quoted in Time-Life Books editors, *Lee Takes Command*. Alexandria, VA: Time-Life Books, 1984.

27. Quoted in Emory Thomas, *Robert E. Lee*. New York: W. W. Norton, 1995.

28. Quoted in Thomas, *Robert E. Lee*.

29. Quoted in Gallagher, *Lee the Soldier*.

30. Quoted in Earle, *Robert E. Lee*.

31. Quoted in Thomas, *Robert E. Lee*.

32. Quoted in Thomas, *Robert E. Lee*.

33. Quoted in Time-Life Books editors, *Lee Takes Command*.

34. Quoted in Earle, *Robert E. Lee*.

35. Quoted in Thomas, *Robert E. Lee*.

36. Quoted in Thomas, *Robert E. Lee*.

37. Quoted in Gallagher, *Lee the Soldier*.

38. Quoted in Davis, *Gray Fox*.

39. Quoted in Davis, *Gray Fox*.

40. Quoted in Dowdy, *Lee*.

41. Quoted in Freeman, *Lee*.

Chapter 3: Thomas J. "Stonewall" Jackson: The Brilliant Fool

42. Quoted in John Bowers, *Stonewall Jackson*. New York: Morrow, 1989.

43. Quoted in Bowers, *Stonewall Jackson*.

44. Quoted in Frank Vandiver, *Mighty Stonewall*. New York: McGraw-Hill, 1957.

45. Quoted in Vandiver, *Mighty Stonewall*.

46. Quoted in James McPherson, *Battle Cry of Freedom*. New York: Oxford University Press, 1988.

47. Quoted in Douglas Southall Freeman, *Lee's Lieutenants*. New York: Charles Scribner's Sons, 1942.

48. Quoted in Vandiver, *Mighty Stonewall*.

49. Quoted in Jonathan Daniels, *Stonewall Jackson*. New York: Random House, 1959.

50. Quoted in Vandiver, *Mighty Stonewall*.

51. Quoted in McPherson, *Battle Cry of Freedom*.

52. Quoted in Freeman, *Lee's Lieutenants*.

53. Quoted in Daniels, *Stonewall Jackson*.

54. Quoted in Daniels, *Stonewall Jackson*.

55. Quoted in Bowers, *Stonewall Jackson*.

56. Quoted in Vandiver, *Mighty Stonewall*.

57. Quoted in G. F. R. Henderson, *Stonewall Jackson and the American Civil War*. New York: Longmans, Green, 1909.

58. Quoted in Henderson, *Stonewall Jackson and the American Civil War*.

59. Quoted in Time-Life Books editors, *The Bloodiest Day*. Alexandria, VA: Time-Life Books, 1984.

60. Quoted in Time-Life Books editors, *The Bloodiest Day*.

61. Quoted in Time-Life Books editors, *Rebels Resurgent*. Alexandria, VA: Time-Life Books, 1985.

62. Quoted in Time-Life Books editors, *Rebels Resurgent*.

63. Quoted in Time-Life Books editors, *Rebels Resurgent*.

64. Quoted in Henderson, *Stonewall Jackson and the American Civil War*.

Chapter 4: James Longstreet: Heroic Villain

65. James Longstreet, *From Manassas to Appomattox*. Bloomington: Indiana University Press, 1960.

66. Longstreet, *From Manassas to Appomattox*.

67. Longstreet, *From Manassas to Appomattox*.

68. Longstreet, *From Manassas to Appomattox*.

69. Quoted in Jeffrey Wert, *General James Longstreet*. New York: Simon and Schuster, 1993.

70. Quoted in Longstreet, *From Manassas to Appomattox*.

71. Quoted in Wert, *General James Longstreet*.

72. Quoted in Longstreet, *From Manassas to Appomattox*.

73. Quoted in Gallagher, *Lee the Soldier.*

74. Longstreet, *From Manassas to Appomattox.*

75. Quoted in H. J. Eckenrode and Bryan Conrad, *James Longstreet: Lee's War Horse.* Chapel Hill: University of North Carolina Press, 1986.

76. Quoted in Eckenrode and Conrad, *James Longstreet.*

77. Quoted in Eckenrode and Conrad, *James Longstreet.*

78. Quoted in Eckenrode and Conrad, *James Longstreet.*

79. Quoted in Eckenrode and Conrad, *James Longstreet.*

80. Quoted in Wert, *General James Longstreet.*

81. Moxley Sorrel, *Recollections of a Confederate Staff Officer.* Jackson, TN: McCowat-Mercer Press, 1958.

82. Quoted in Wert, *General James Longstreet.*

83. Quoted in Eckenrode and Conrad, *James Longstreet.*

84. Longstreet, *From Manassas to Appomattox.*

85. Longstreet, *From Manassas to Appomattox.*

86. Longstreet, *From Manassas to Appomattox.*

87. Longstreet, *From Manassas to Appomattox.*

88. Quoted in Wert, *General James Longstreet.*

89. Quoted in Wert, *General James Longstreet.*

Chapter 5: James Ewell Brown Stuart: The Happy Cavalier

90. Quoted in Freeman, *Lee's Lieutenants.*

91. Quoted in Freeman, *Lee's Lieutenants.*

92. Quoted in Freeman, *Lee's Lieutenants.*

93. Quoted in Freeman, *Lee's Lieutenants.*

94. Quoted in Emory Thomas, *Bold Dragoon.* New York: Harper & Row, 1986.

95. Quoted in Thomas, *Bold Dragoon.*

96. Quoted in Thomas, *Bold Dragoon.*

97. Quoted in Freeman, *Lee's Lieutenants.*

98. Quoted in Thomas, *Bold Dragoon.*

99. Quoted in Burke Davis, *Jeb Stuart.* New York: Rinehart, 1957.

100. Quoted in Davis, *Jeb Stuart.*

101. Quoted in Davis, *Jeb Stuart.*

102. Quoted in Freeman, *Lee's Lieutenants.*

103. Quoted in Thomas, *Bold Dragoon.*

104. Quoted in Davis, *Jeb Stuart.*

105. Quoted in Thomas, *Bold Dragoon.*

106. Quoted in Thomas, *Bold Dragoon.*

107. Quoted in Davis, *Jeb Stuart.*

108. Quoted in Davis, *Jeb Stuart.*

109. Quoted in Freeman, *Lee's Lieutenants.*

110. Quoted in Mark Nesbitt, *Saber and Scapegoat.* Mechanicsburg, PA: Stackpole Books, 1994.

111. Quoted in Nesbitt, *Saber and Scapegoat.*

112. Quoted in Nesbitt, *Saber and Scapegoat.*

113. Quoted in Gordon Rhea, *The Road to Yellow Tavern.* Baton Rouge: Louisiana State University Press, 1997.

Chapter 6: Nathan Bedford Forrest: The Best and the Worst

114. Quoted in Brian Wills, *A Battle from the Start: The Life of Nathan Bedford Forrest.* New York: HarperCollins, 1992.

115. Quoted in Wills, *A Battle from the Start.*

116. Quoted in Wills, *A Battle from the Start.*

117. Quoted in Wills, *A Battle from the Start.*

118. Quoted in Thomson Jordon et al., *The Campaigns of Lieut. Gen. N. B. Forrest and Forrest's Cavalry.* New York: Da Capo Press, 1996.

119. Quoted in Jack Hurst, *Nathan Bedford Forrest: A Biography.* New York: Vintage Books, 1994.

120. Quoted in Hurst, *Nathan Bedford Forrest.*

121. Quoted in Hurst, *Nathan Bedford Forrest.*

122. Quoted in Hurst, *Nathan Bedford Forrest.*

123. Quoted in Jordon et al., *The Campaigns of Lieut. Gen. N. B. Forrest.*

124. Quoted in John Allan Wyeth, *The Life of Nathan Bedford Forrest.* New York: Book Sales, 1996.

125. Quoted in Wyeth, *The Life of Nathan Bedford Forrest.*

126. Quoted in Hurst, *Nathan Bedford Forrest.*

127. Quoted in Andrew Nelson Lytle, *Bedford Forrest and His Critter Company.* Nashville: J. S. Sanders, 1992.

128. Quoted in Jordon et al., *The Campaigns of Lieut. Gen. N. B. Forrest.*

129. Quoted in Wyeth, *The Life of Nathan Bedford Forrest.*

130. Quoted in John Allan Wyeth, *That Devil Forrest.* Baton Rouge: Louisiana State University, 1991.

131. Quoted in Wyeth, *That Devil Forrest.*

132. Quoted in Wyeth, *That Devil Forrest.*

133. Quoted in Wyeth, *That Devil Forrest.*

134. Quoted in Wyeth, *The Life of Nathan Bedford Forrest.*

135. Quoted in Lytle, *Bedford Forrest and His Critter Company.*

136. Quoted in Jordon et al., *The Campaigns of Lieut. Gen. N. B. Forrest.*

137. Quoted in Jordon et al., *The Campaigns of Lieut. Gen. N. B. Forrest.*

138. Quoted in Wyeth, *The Life of Nathan Bedford Forrest.*

139. Quoted in Wyeth, *That Devil Forrest.*

140. Quoted in Wyeth, *That Devil Forrest.*

141. Quoted in Lytle, *Bedford Forrest and His Critter Company.*

142. Quoted in Hurst, *Nathan Bedford Forrest.*

143. Quoted in Jordon et al., *The Campaigns of Lieut. Gen. N. B. Forrest.*

144. Quoted in Wyeth, *That Devil Forrest.*

145. Quoted in Wyeth, *That Devil Forrest.*

146. Quoted in Lytle, *Bedford Forrest and His Critter Company.*

147. Quoted in Lytle, *Bedford Forrest and His Critter Company.*

148. Quoted in John Marszalek, *Sherman: A Soldier's Passion for Order.* New York: Free Press, 1993.

149. *The War of the Rebellion: A Compilation of the Official Records of the Union and Confederate Armies.* Washington, DC: U.S. Government Printing Office, 1880–1901.

150. Quoted in *The War of the Rebellion.*

151. Quoted in Hurst, *Nathan Bedford Forrest.*

152. Quoted in Jordon et al., *The Campaigns of Lieut. Gen. N. B. Forrest.*

153. Quoted in Lytle, *Bedford Forrest and His Critter Company.*

154. Quoted in Hurst, *Nathan Bedford Forrest.*

155. Quoted in Hurst, *Nathan Bedford Forrest.*

156. Quoted in Lytle, *Bedford Forrest and His Critter Company.*

157. Quoted in Wyeth, *That Devil Forrest.*

158. Quoted in Marszalek, *Sherman.*

159. Quoted in Wyeth, *That Devil Forrest.*

160. Quoted in Wyeth, *That Devil Forrest.*

161. Quoted in Jordon et al., *The Campaigns of Lieut. Gen. N. B. Forrest.*

162. Quoted in Lytle, *Bedford Forrest and His Critter Company.*

163. Quoted in Hurst, *Nathan Bedford Forrest.*

164. Quoted in Wyeth, *That Devil Forrest.*

165. Quoted in Wyeth, *The Life of Nathan Bedford Forrest.*

166. Quoted in Wyeth, *That Devil Forrest.*

167. Quoted in Hurst, *Nathan Bedford Forrest.*

168. Quoted in Wyeth, *The Life of Nathan Bedford Forrest.*

169. Quoted in Wyeth, *The Life of Nathan Bedford Forrest.*

170. Quoted in Lytle, *Bedford Forrest and His Critter Company.*

171. Quoted in Wyeth, *That Devil Forrest.*

172. Quoted in Wyeth, *That Devil Forrest.*

CHRONOLOGY

Pre–Civil War Era

1820
Missouri Compromise.

1846
Mexican War/Wilmot Proviso.

1850
Compromise of 1850.

1854
Kansas-Nebraska Act.

1859
John Brown's raid on Harpers Ferry.

1860
Abraham Lincoln elected president of the United States; South Carolina secedes from the Union.

Civil War

1861
January
Mississippi, Florida, Alabama, Georgia, Louisiana, and Texas secede.

February
Confederate States of America formed; Jefferson Davis elected president.

April
Virginia, Arkansas, Tennessee, and North Carolina secede.

April 12
Confederates fire on Fort Sumter.

April 14
Fort Sumter falls.

April 15
Lincoln calls for seventy-five thousand volunteers to put down the rebellion.

July 21
First Battle of Manassas (Bull Run).

August 10
Battle of Wilson's Creek, Missouri (Confederate victory).

1862

January
Lee's Cheat Mountain campaign in western Virginia (now West Virginia).

February 12–16
Fall of Fort Donelson in Tennessee.

April 6–7
Battle of Shiloh, Tennessee.

May–June
Jackson's Shenadoah Valley campaign.

May
Virginia Peninsula campaign.

May 31–June 1
Battle of Fair Oaks.

June 12–15
Stuart's ride around McClellan on Virginia Peninsula.

June 26–July 2
Seven Days' Battle in Virginia (Mechanicsville, Gaines' Mill, White Oak Swamp, Malvern Hill).

July
Forrest's first raid through Tennessee (including capture of federal garrison at Murfreesboro).

August 22–23
Stuart's raid on Catlett's Station.

August 28
Battle of Groveton near Manassas, Virginia.

August 29–30
Second Battle of Manassas, Virginia.

September 17
Battle of Antietam, Maryland.

October 10–11
Stuart's Chambersburg Raid through Maryland and Pennsylvania.

December 13
Battle of Fredericksburg, Virginia.

December 11–January 3
Forrest's second raid through Tennessee (including the Battle of Parker's Crossroads).

1863

January 1
Emancipation Proclamation takes effect.

April 11–May 3
Streight's raid through northern Alabama (Forrest captures Federals on May 3).

May 2–4
Battle of Chancellorsville, Virginia.

May 22
Siege of Vicksburg, Mississippi, begins.

June 9
Battle of Brandy Station in Virginia.

June 24–July 3
Stuart's Gettysburg raid through Virginia, Maryland, and Pennsylvania.

July 1–4
Battle of Gettysburg.

July 4
Vicksburg falls.

September 19–20
Battle of Chickamauga, Georgia and Tennessee.

November–December
Longstreet's Knoxville campaign in eastern Tennessee.

November 23–25
Battles of Lookout Mountain and Missionary Ridge at Chattanooga, Tennessee.

1864
April 12
Battle of Fort Pillow in Tennessee.

May 5–6
Battle of the Wilderness in Virginia.

May 7
Sherman's march through Georgia begins.

May 8–12
Battle of Spotsylvania in Virginia.

May 11
Battle of Yellow Tavern in Virginia.

June 1–3
Battle of Cold Harbor, Virginia.

June 10
Battle of Brice's Crossroads in Mississippi.

June 15
Siege of Petersburg, Virginia, begins.

September 2
Atlanta falls to Sherman.

November 14
Sherman begins march to the sea in Georgia.

December 15–16
Battle of Nashville, Tennessee.

December 22
Sherman takes Savannah, Georgia.

1865
February 18
Charleston, South Carolina, falls.

April 2
Lee moves out of Petersburg.

April 3
Richmond, Virginia, falls.

April 9
Lee surrenders at Appomattox Court House, Virginia.

FOR FURTHER READING

Barbara J. Bennett, *Stonewall Jackson: Lee's Greatest Lieutenant.* Parsippany, NJ: Silver Burdett, 1991. Bennett devotes the text to the positive aspects of Jackson's character (such as his honesty, courage, and single-mindedness) without spending equal time on the "negative" (his intolerance, stubbornness, and aloofness). Still, an effective rendering of the enigmatic general and how he shaped the Civil War. Maps illuminate campaigns.

Edward F. Dolan, *American Civil War: A House Divided.* Brookfield, CT: Millbrook, 1997. Another concise and well-rounded history of the war. This work has the distinction of enlightening the reader regarding the personal attributes of the commanders involved (as well as blacks, women, civilians, and the common soldier). Maps and sidebars illuminate the narrative.

Cathy East Dubroski, *Robert E. Lee and the Rise of the South* (The History of the Civil War). Parsippany, NJ: Silver Burdett Press, 1991. Not just another biography of the over-biographied Lee. This account focuses not only on the Confederate commander's life and achievements but on the life and achievements of the Confederacy in general. The parallel highs and lows of both the man and his country offer striking similarities and suggest that the fortunes of each were inextricably meshed with those of the other.

Dan Harmon, *Civil War Generals* (Looking Into the Past, Peoples, Places, and Customs). New York: Chelsea House, 1998. Short biographies of the greatest Northern and Southern generals of the Civil War. Due to the brevity of each life story, many pertinent facts and anecdotes are left out. For a quick glimpse of these men, however, the author does a creditable job.

Mona Kerby, *Robert E. Lee: Southern Hero of the Civil War.* New York: Enslow, 1997. The author offers an overwhelmingly positive view of the Confederacy's top military commander, girding the legend of the "Marble Man" without showing any of his flaws. Little is said of his failed campaigns in western Virginia during 1861 or his imprudent charges at Gettysburg and Petersburg. All in all, though, this work provides a lasting impression of the "Gray Fox."

Delia Ray, *Behind the Blue and Gray: The Soldiers' Life in the Civil War.* New York: Lodestar Books, 1991. The author convincingly establishes a connection between young Civil War soldiers and the youth of today. Helps modern students understand why the study of the war has relevance for them.

James I. Robertson, *Civil War!: America Becomes One Nation*. New York: Knopf, 1992. Probably the most scholarly of all young adult histories of the Civil War. The author eloquently argues that the horrors of the war served a positive purpose in the end. They united the states with a commitment never to be separated again and solidified the previously fledgling regions into a singular power with which the world's political establishment would have to reckon. Many maps, charts, and diagrams.

Julian Segal, *Civil War Almanac*. New York: Lowell House, 1997. This near-encyclopedic work contains a wealth of information not only on the Confederate generals but on every other aspect of the war as well. Especially helpful for the reluctant reader who needs short, high-interest "factoids" to ponder before moving quickly to the next.

Major Works Consulted

John Bowers, *Stonewall Jackson*. New York: Morrow, 1989. Unsensational narrative written for the layman looking for a general introduction to Jackson and his times. Helpful maps and diagrams.

Jonathan Daniels, *Stonewall Jackson*. New York: Random House, 1959. Provides sufficient background material on the era, war, and man to enlighten even new initiates to Civil War history. Written perhaps a little too rapidly to satisfy the expected hunger for Civil War literature at the beginning of the Civil War centennial celebrations.

Burke Davis, *Gray Fox: Robert E. Lee and the Civil War*. New York: Rinehart, 1956. Satisfying blend of academic research and high readability. Scholarly work written with a dramatic flair.

———, *Jeb Stuart*. New York: Rinehart, 1957. Companion to the previous work. Both offerings to the "intelligent layman." Clear maps. Revealing sketches and photos.

David Donald, *The Civil War and Reconstruction*. Lexington, MA: Heath, 1969. Provides ardent Civil War enthusiasts with an in-depth study of military, political, and sociological aspects of the period. An interesting and appreciated Southern perspective occasionally seeps through.

Clifford Dowdy, *Lee*. New York: Little, Brown, 1965. Another effective crossover between academic and general literature. Little new offered, however.

H. J. Eckenrode and Bryan Conrad, *James Longstreet: Lee's War Horse*. Chapel Hill: University of North Carolina Press, 1986. More emphasis here on scholarship than on general readability but a gold mine of information on an underreported subject for those willing to dig.

Douglas Southall Freeman, *Lee*. New York: Collier, 1993. A distillation of several volumes. The author remains the unchallenged authority on Robert E. Lee.

———, *Lee's Lieutenants*. New York: Charles Scribner's Sons, 1942. A revered classic and principal source for dozens of biographers who followed.

John A. Garraty, *The American Nation*. New York: Harper & Row, 1971. Thorough and insightful survey of American history. Used widely as a university text. Sidebarlike "portfolios" broaden understanding. Many maps, photos, illustrations.

G. F. R. Henderson, *Stonewall Jackson and the American Civil War.* New York: Longmans, Green, 1909. Another classic, this one written by a British professional soldier who, perhaps, grew a bit too fond of his subject. Sift for Jackson's flaws.

Jack Hurst, *Nathan Bedford Forrest: A Biography.* New York: Vintage Books, 1994. One of several accounts to grow out of Forrest's recent emergence from the dustbin of history. Balanced, thoughtful, complete. Insightful collection of photos, sketches.

James Longstreet, *From Manassas to Appomattox.* Bloomington: Indiana University Press, 1960. From the horse's mouth, an entertaining and provocative autobiography, which, like all autobiographies, must be read critically and compared with other literature.

James McPherson, *Battle Cry of Freedom.* New York: Oxford University Press, 1988. Academic yet reasonably readable survey of the Civil War era with an emphasis on the political, economic, and sociological factors as opposed to purely military ones. Not a "war story."

Emory Thomas, *Bold Dragoon.* New York: Harper & Row, 1986. Perhaps the definitive modern work on Stuart. Certainly illuminates all significant areas of the cavalryman's life and does so in an entertaining manner.

Frank Vandiver, *Mighty Stonewall.* New York: McGraw-Hill, 1957. Excellent overview of the general's life, both early and adult. However, tends to downplay his quirky personality in favor of that of the more conventional "warrior image."

Jeffrey Wert, *General James Longstreet.* New York: Simon and Schuster, 1992. Particularly even account of Longstreet's life. Underscores the controversial man's successes while not glossing over his considerable failings.

Brian Wills, *A Battle from the Start: The Life of Nathan Bedford Forrest.* New York: HarperCollins, 1992. Tends toward glamorizing a sometimes barbaric man but then what is war if not barbarism? And who should be glamorized if not war's most colorful practitioners? Fairly handles his legendary mistreatment of blacks.

John Allan Wyeth, *The Life of Nathan Bedford Forrest.* New York: Book Sales, 1996. Explains, without attempting to justify, how Forrest's upbringing and times led both to his magnificence as a combat soldier and his indifference to the suffering of his enemies. Particularly insightful handling of his Ku Klux Klan days.

ADDITIONAL WORKS CONSULTED

David Chandler, *The Campaigns of Napoleon*. New York: Macmillan, 1966.

Mary Boykin Chesnut, *A Diary from Dixie*. Cambridge, MA: Harvard University Press, 1980.

Henry Steele Commager, *America's Robert E. Lee*. Lakeville, CT: Castle Press, 1991.

Henry Kyd Douglas, *I Rode With Stonewall*. New York: Mockingbird Books, 1979.

Gwynne Dyer, *War*. New York: Crown, 1985.

Peter Earle, *Robert E. Lee*. New York: Saturday Review Press, 1974.

Gary W. Gallagher, ed., *Lee the Soldier*. Lincoln: University of Nebraska Press, 1996.

Eugene Genovese, *The World the Slaveholders Made*. New York: Pantheon Books, 1969.

William D. Halsey and Louis Shores, eds., *Merit Students' Encyclopedia*. Vol. 4. New York: Macmillan Educational, 1976.

Thomson Jordon et al., *The Campaigns of Lieut. Gen. N. B. Forrest and Forrest's Cavalry*. New York: Da Capo Press, 1996.

Helen Gortch Longstreet, *Lee and Longstreet at High Tide*. Reprint. Wilmington, NC: Broadfoot Publishing Co., 1989.

Andrew Nelson Lytle, *Bedford Forrest and His Critter Company*. Nashville: J. S. Sanders, 1992.

John Marszalek, *Sherman: A Soldier's Passion for Order*. New York: Free Press, 1993.

Eric McKitirick, *Slavery Defended: The Views of the Old South*. Englewood Cliffs, NJ: Prentice-Hall, 1963.

Mark Nesbitt, *Saber and Scapegoat*. Mechanicsburg, PA: Stackpole Books, 1994.

Gordon Rhea, *The Road to Yellow Tavern*. Baton Rouge: Louisiana State University Press, 1997.

Moxley Sorrel, *Recollections of a Confederate Staff Officer*. Jackson, TN: McCowat-Mercer Press, 1958.

Emory Thomas, *Robert E. Lee*. New York: W. W. Norton, 1995.

Time-Life Books editors, *The Bloodiest Day*. Alexandria, VA: Time-Life Books, 1984.

————, *Lee Takes Command*. Alexandria, VA: Time-Life Books, 1984.

————, *Rebels Resurgent*. Alexandria, VA: Time-Life Books, 1985.

John Allan Wyeth, *That Devil Forrest*. Baton Rouge: Louisiana State University, 1991.

The War of the Rebellion: A Compilation of the Official Records of the Union and Confederate Armies. Washington, DC: U.S. Government Printing Office, 1880–1901.

New Orleans, Longstreet's years in, 78–79

Northerners
  contrasted with Southerners, 11–12, 16
  monopolize trade, 14
  trades and skills of, 11–12
  upper class, 16

Official Records of the Union Army, 115–16

Operation Desert Storm, 61

Parker's Crossroad, 111–12
Patton, George S., 61, 119
Persian Gulf War, 61
Pickett, George, 52
Pickett's Charge, 41, 62, 76
Pope, John, 34, 71, 91–92

Reconstruction, 78–80
Richmond County Academy, 64
Rommel, Erwin, 61, 119

Sansom, Emma, 114
Schwarzkopf, Norman, 61
Scott, Winfield, 21, 26–28, 52
Seven Days' battle, 32–34, 70
Seven Pines, Battle of, 33, 70
Sharpsburg. *See* Antietam, Battle of
Shenandoah campaign, 55–56
Sherman, William T., 115, 119
Shiloh, Battle of, 102–103, 110
slavery
  aristocrats' views towards, 15–16
  Forrest's views on, 107, 111, 122
  Jackson's views on, 55
  Lee's views on, 25, 37
  Lincoln's views on, 16
Southerners
  agricultural strengths of, 12–14
  contrasted with Northerners, 11–12, 16
  dependence on Northern economy, 14
  middle class, 14–15
  secede from Union, 17
  upper class, 15–16
Spotsylvania, Battle of, 98
Streight, Abel D., 112–14
Stuart, Flora Cooke, 87
Stuart, James Ewell Brown (J. E. B.), 82–101

blamed for Gettysburg defeat, 101
childhood of, 85
combative nature of, 85
daughter's death, 95
devotion to family, 90, 92, 97
legacy after death, 100–101
lures Maryland to Rebel causes, 92–93
marriage and children of, 87
military blunders of, 94, 96
military courage of, 88–89
military roles
  at Antietam, 93–94
  in Chancellorsville campaign, 95
  at First Battle of Manassas, 89
  at Gettysburg, 96–98, 101
  at Harpers Ferry, 29, 87
  in Pope's headquarters raid, 91–92
  in rides around McClellan's troops, 82–84, 94
  at Second Battle of Manassas, 92
  in Yankee gunboat raid, 90–91
nickname, 9, 86
resigns from U.S. Army, 88
West Point education of, 29, 85–86
wounding and death of, 99–100

tariffs, 14
technology, in North, 12
Toombs, Robert, 71

Union, free and slave states in, 16–18
Union generals. *See specific generals*
Union troops, violence of, 19, 115–16
United States Military Academy. *See* West Point
upper class, in North and South, 15–16

Vera Cruz, Mexico, 27
Virginia Military Institute, 54–55

Washington, George, 22
Washington College, 45
West Point
  famous alumni of, 52
  Jackson's years at, 49–52
  Lee's years at, 23–24, 28
  Longstreet's years at, 64–65
  Stuart's years at, 29, 85–86
Wilderness, Battle of the, 76–77, 98
Wilmot Proviso, 16–17

PICTURE CREDITS

ABOUT THE AUTHOR

James P. Reger hails from a West Virginia family whose history parallels that of America's itself. One of his ancestors fought with Jeb Stuart's cavalry at Gettysburg; another with Stonewall Jackson's infantry at Antietam. A third died in a Northern prison camp. Surrounded by battlefields and other reminders of the war, Reger grew up listening to the ancestral wartime lore passed down by grandparents and great-uncles whose own parents, uncles, and cousins had endured the hardships firsthand.

He formalized his study of Civil War history at West Virginia University and went on to teach social studies, English, and special education at the secondary level. When not teaching, reenacting, or performing Civil War living history sketches for school audiences, Mr. Reger resides with his wife and young son in a coastal suburb of San Diego, California.